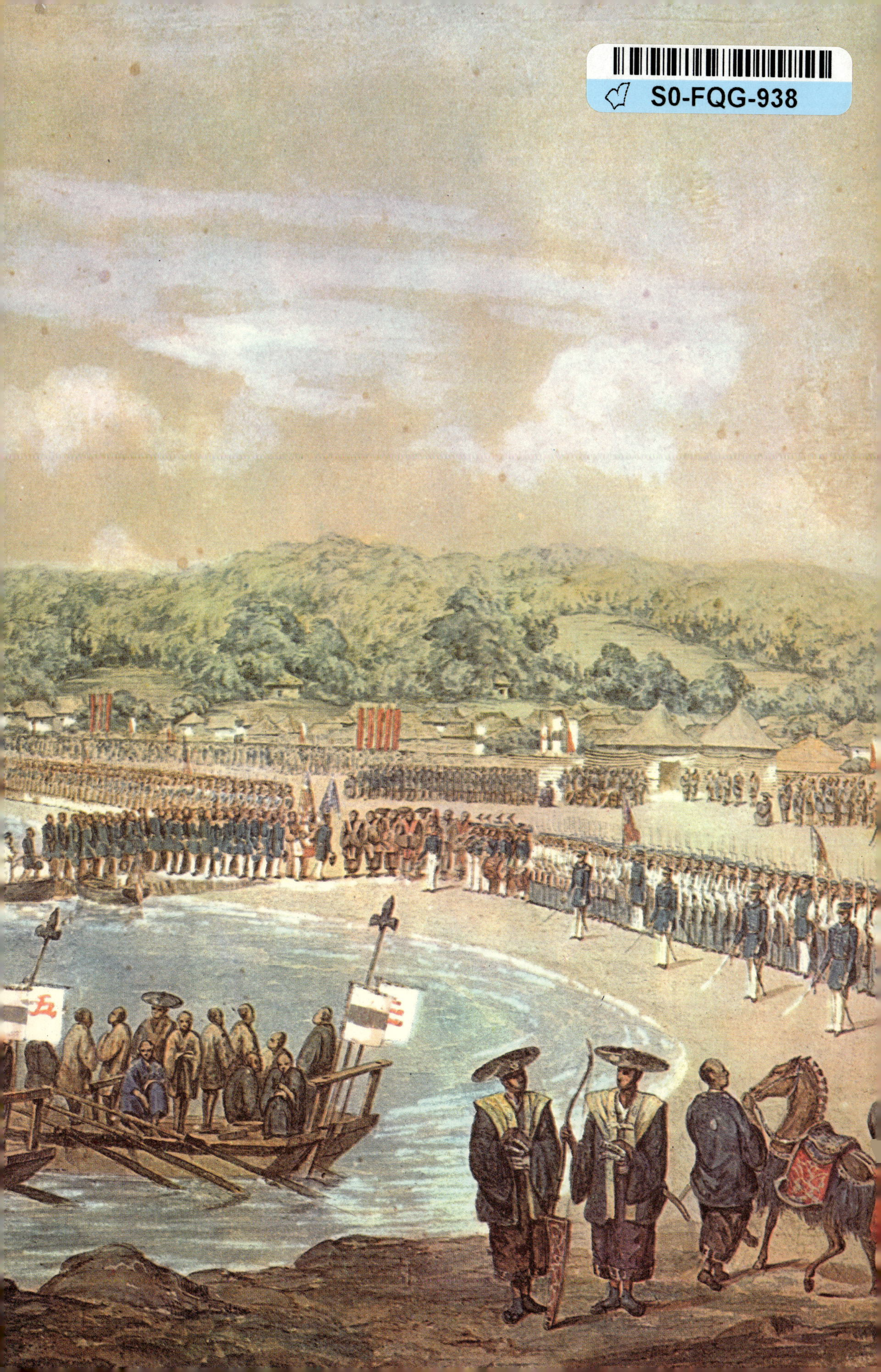

COMMODORE

FIRST EDITION

© 1963 by American Heritage Publishing Co., Inc., 551 Fifth Avenue, New York 17, New York. All rights reserved under Berne and Pan-American Copyright Conventions. Library of Congress Catalog Card Number: 63-20168.

PERRY IN JAPAN

BY THE EDITORS OF
AMERICAN HERITAGE
The Magazine of History

AUTHOR
ROBERT L. REYNOLDS

CONSULTANT
DOUGLAS MacARTHUR II
Former U.S. Ambassador to Japan

PUBLISHED BY
**AMERICAN HERITAGE
PUBLISHING CO., INC.,**
New York

BOOK TRADE AND INSTITUTIONAL DISTRIBUTION BY
HARPER & ROW

亞墨利加人

Foreword

"The honor of the nation calls for it, and the interest of commerce demands it." Tough, stiff-collared Commodore Matthew Calbraith Perry wrote these words aboard the steam warship *Mississippi* on his way to Japan in 1853, describing the reasons behind his historic expedition.

If by "honor" Perry meant national interest, he was assuredly right. Great Britain and Russia were both active in the western Pacific in the mid-nineteenth century; unless the United States acted fast, she would find herself without influence in that part of the world. In fact, just four months after Perry landed in Japan, a Russian squadron of four ships sailed into the port of Nagasaki. By then the Americans had already begun trying—by diplomatic tact and naval threats—to pry open the door that the Japanese empire had locked against the outside world.

There was no doubt as to what Perry meant by the "interest of commerce." When he departed for the Orient in 1853, United States trade with China was already worth $19 million a year, and Japan promised an equally lucrative market. A New Orleans journal brashly guessed that it might amount to $200 million annually. The nation was indeed looking westward for reasons of pride and profit as Perry sailed.

This book is the story of America's first major overseas adventure—a journey to a virtually unknown part of the world (Perry had to pay $30,000 to Dutch traders for unreliable charts of Japanese waters). Fortunately a wealth of official and unofficial material exists in which the daily events of the expedition are recorded. As is evident from the contemporary pictures on the following pages, Perry's squadron fired the imaginations of Japanese artists who had never before seen such awesome ships that belched smoke, or such bizarre weapons and uniforms.

A vivid and important first chapter in America's international history has thus been preserved. How America and Japan would fare in their future relations with each other and with the world is, however, another story.
—The Editors

Soon after Perry opened Japan for trade, a Japanese artist painted this picture of an American merchant family.

Six new AMERICAN HERITAGE JUNIOR LIBRARY *books are published each year. Titles currently available are:*

COMMODORE PERRY IN JAPAN
THE BATTLE OF GETTYSBURG
ANDREW JACKSON, SOLDIER AND STATESMAN
ADVENTURES IN THE WILDERNESS
LEXINGTON, CONCORD AND BUNKER HILL
CLIPPER SHIPS AND CAPTAINS
D-DAY, THE INVASION OF EUROPE
WESTWARD ON THE OREGON TRAIL
THE FRENCH AND INDIAN WARS
GREAT DAYS OF THE CIRCUS
STEAMBOATS ON THE MISSISSIPPI
COWBOYS AND CATTLE COUNTRY
TEXAS AND THE WAR WITH MEXICO
THE PILGRIMS AND PLYMOUTH COLONY
THE CALIFORNIA GOLD RUSH
PIRATES OF THE SPANISH MAIN
TRAPPERS AND MOUNTAIN MEN
MEN OF SCIENCE AND INVENTION
NAVAL BATTLES AND HEROES
THOMAS JEFFERSON AND HIS WORLD
DISCOVERERS OF THE NEW WORLD
RAILROADS IN THE DAYS OF STEAM
INDIANS OF THE PLAINS
THE STORY OF YANKEE WHALING

American Heritage also publishes HORIZON CARAVEL BOOKS, *a similar series on world history, culture, and the arts. Titles currently available are:*

THE SEARCH FOR EARLY MAN
JOAN OF ARC
EXPLORATION OF AFRICA
NELSON AND THE AGE OF FIGHTING SAIL
ALEXANDER THE GREAT
RUSSIA UNDER THE CZARS
HEROES OF POLAR EXPLORATION
KNIGHTS OF THE CRUSADES

COVER: *The great confrontation—a Japanese artist painted Perry, stiffly erect in his dress blues, meeting the high commissioners at Uraga in 1853.*
U.S. NAVAL ACADEMY MUSEUM

FRONT ENDSHEET: *Wilhelm Heine's official painting of the Uraga landing shows American officers stepping out of the boats, hats in their hands.*
COLLECTION OF J. WILLIAM MIDDENDORF II

BACK ENDSHEET: *These Navy officers participate, rather doubtfully, in a formal, Japanese-style banquet held during the 1854 treaty negotiations.*
BOEHRINGER COLLECTION; MARINERS MUSEUM

Contents

Old Matt's silhouette is emblazoned on a shield in this allegorical scene.

1	Black Ships off Japan	10
2	Behind the Closed Door	22
3	Old Matt Takes Command	48
4	The President's Letter	66
5	"All the Same Heart"	88
6	The Open Door	122
	Acknowledgments	148
	For Further Reading	149
	Index	150

ILLUSTRATED WITH PAINTINGS, PRINTS, PHOTOGRAPHS, DRAWINGS, AND MAPS OF THE PERIOD

1

Commodore Perry's black-hulled fleet, carrying the "Gospel of God" and more than a hundred guns to uphold it, pounds through heavy seas toward the forbidden shores of Japan.

BLACK SHIPS OFF JAPAN

Aboard the United States steam frigate *Susquehanna*, sailing through the northwest Pacific Ocean on a July morning in 1853, drums and fifes imperiously sounded "general quarters." Officers ran to their stations. Sailors armed with cutlasses and pikes trotted up and down the holystoned decks, ready to repel boarders. Gunports snapped open; cannon were run in, loaded, and run out again while gunners with lighted matches stood by to touch them off. Behind the guns, U.S. marines formed in solid ranks, loaded their muskets, and awaited the order to fire. Pumps were manned, and fire-control parties assembled to deal with damage to be expected from enemy action.

On the quarter-deck, surveying the scene through eyes that missed nothing, stood Commodore Matthew Calbraith Perry, whose broad command pennant fluttered from the *Susquehanna*'s masthead. He could see similar preparations going on aboard the other ships of his squadron—the steamer *Mississippi*, which had brought him to the Orient, and the sloops *Plymouth* and *Saratoga*. Ahead lay the main islands of Japan, to which he had been sent to negotiate a treaty of friendship and commerce. "Make no use of force," the Secretary of State had ordered, "except in the last resort for defense, if attacked. . . ."

But Japan had been closed to the outside world for 250 years. American vessels attempting to approach her had been rebuffed, and one—an unarmed merchant brig—had been fired upon. Even castaways from Yankee whalers wrecked off the Japanese coast had been imprisoned.

Perry, not knowing what was in store for him, was determined to be prepared for any occurrence. As the retreat from general quarters was sounded and the drill—for drill it was—came to an end, he could be satisfied; he was certain that, should their reception be violent, he and his men would give a good account of themselves.

What lay behind the bold journey of the *Susquehanna* and her sister ships? Why had the most prominent officer in the Navy been ordered to steam more than halfway around the globe, bearing a letter from the President of the United States to the emperor of a country that obviously wanted nothing to do with America and the Western world?

There were substantial reasons. The United States by 1853 had grown from a child to a strong young giant, confident and cocky, eager to flex its muscles. In 1800 its population of less than five and a half million had huddled along the narrow strip of land between

In the mid-nineteenth century the water front of San Francisco (below) was crowded; Americans were moving West. Spokesmen for "Manifest Destiny," who had been urging that the country expand to its fullest, now looked beyond the Golden Gate to the vast emptiness of the Pacific. This spirit of expansion was one of the forces that brought about the historic meeting of Commodore Perry and representatives of the emperor of Japan.

NEW-YORK HISTORICAL SOCIETY

Commodore Perry   *Emperor Komei*

the Alleghenies and the sea. By 1853 there were over twenty-three million Americans; by purchase and conquest, and driven by their own natural restlessness, they had pushed across the continent to achieve what they believed to be their "Manifest Destiny."

This great westward movement picked up speed as the nineteenth century matured. First, in 1803, had come the Louisiana Purchase, through which Thomas Jefferson, cursed by many for his folly, had added to the national domain a rich territory from which eight entire states and most of five others would be carved. Texas was annexed in 1845, and the boundaries of Oregon were agreed upon with England in 1846. Then, as a result of victory in the Mexican War—in which Matthew Calbraith Perry had first been recognized as a national hero—the United States acquired California and the rest of the Southwest down to the Gila River and the Rio Grande.

Even as Perry now approached Japan, James Gadsden of South Carolina was in Mexico negotiating the purchase of land in Arizona and New Mexico which would round out the southwestern boundaries of the United States. The discovery of gold in California in 1849—and the westward rush of thousands upon thousands of Americans to get rich quick—meant that even that extreme outpost would not long remain an unpeopled wilderness.

Nor would the drive toward expansion stop at the ocean's edge. "The

Among the principal architects of westward expansion during the early 1850's was President Millard Fillmore, who strikes a commanding pose in the portrait by G. P. A. Healy at right. As Secretary of State in Fillmore's cabinet, the aging but eloquent Daniel Webster (above) won support in Congress for the drive to pry open Japan's closed ports.

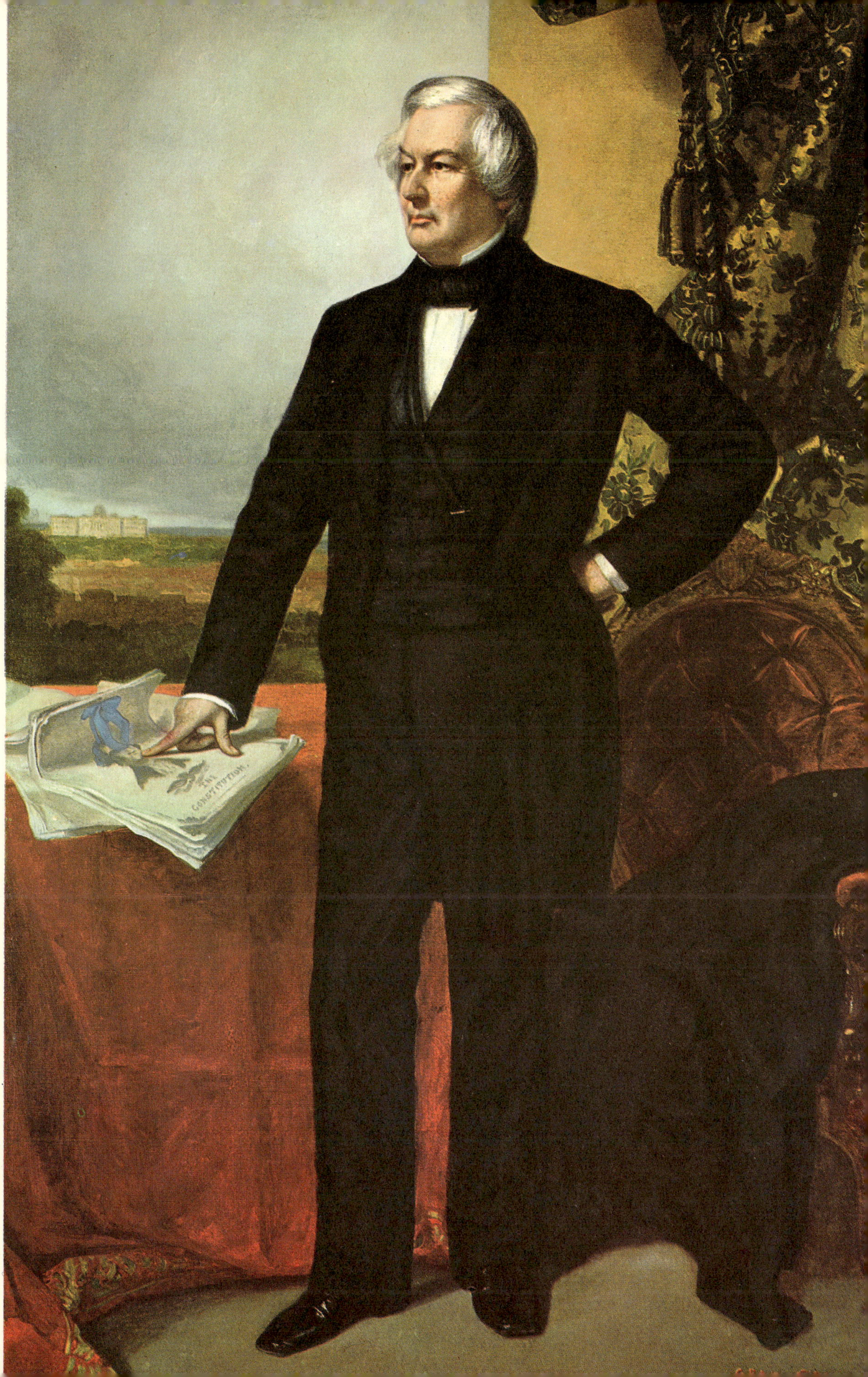

THE WHITE HOUSE

Americans were driven ever farther across the Pacific by their need for seal and whale oil. Sealing grounds nearer home were wiped out quickly, although as seen in this painting, the methods of slaughter were crude.

... destiny of the American people," wrote one of expansion's prophets, "is to subdue the continent . . . to animate the many hundred millions of its people and to cheer them upward . . . to regenerate superannuated nations . . . to teach old nations a new civilization . . . and shed blessings around the world. Divine task! Immortal mission! Let us tread fast and joyfully the open trail before us." The giant had grown to full size, facing "superannuated" Japan from the opposite shores of the broad Pacific and looking for new worlds to conquer.

Since 1820 Yankee whalers had been active in the western Pacific, although they were sorely hampered by the lack of friendly harbors in Japan. Fleets operated from the Hawaiian Islands and had to endure the hazards of traversing the world's broadest ocean. The opening of Japanese ports would provide bases and shelter close to the whaling grounds. And it would assure humane treatment to American castaways (and deserters), who had been so inhospitably greeted in the past.

Ports in Japan would be a boon for traders as well. Already, commerce with China had become big business,

About 1854 artist George Chinnery painted these clippers and side-wheel steamers anchored at Hong Kong, which with China's other major treaty ports at Shanghai and Canton, handled a huge volume of Yankee trade.

worth millions even as early as 1820. Seal skins from America's northwest coast were the support of the China trade at this time, for they were highly prized by the Chinese merchants. In the 1840's fast clipper ships, the glory of the American merchant marine, brought raw materials and manufactured goods like textiles around the Cape of Good Hope and across the Indian Ocean to be sold in Hong Kong, Canton, and Shanghai. Then the tall ships crowded on sail again and skimmed swiftly across the Pacific, laden with products of the exotic East—silks, teas, and spices—to be sold in America.

But the lovely clippers had seen their best days, as the presence of the two smoke-belching frigates in Perry's squadron testified; the Navy and the merchant fleet were switching to steam. Like the northward expansion of the whaling industry, this change had a direct bearing on Perry's mission, and was in fact a major reason for it. The inefficient engines of the new ocean-going steamers burned enormous quantities of coal, which had to be transported in special vessels, called colliers, all the way from ports in the United States—or from

A Protestant missionary preaches the word of God to the peoples of the world. Some churchmen maintained that certain passages in the Bible proved America was "chosen" to spread Christianity among the Japanese.

Wales—to depots along the China coast. Japan, it was rumored, had extensive deposits of coal; these seemed to Secretary of State Daniel Webster "a gift of Providence, deposited by the Creator of all things in the depths of the Japanese islands for the benefit of the human family."

American politicians did talk that way in the 1850's; it was a religious age. Moreover, it was an age in which commerce and the Gospel went hand-in-hand. The first permanent American foothold in Hawaii had been gained by New England missionaries in 1820; their descendants were to remain influential in the islands down to the time Hawaii became our fiftieth state, a goal the missionaries did much to advance.

In the drive across the Pacific and toward Japan the desire to convert the heathen to Protestant Christianity was certainly very strong. Americans were convinced that the Japanese were sunk in "the grossest paganism" and wallowing in immorality. True, a considerable number of them had been converted to Christianity in the sixteenth century, but the missionaries had been Roman Catholic priests from Spain and Portugal. To American Protestants, that did not count as pure Christianity.

All these factors—commercial, national, and religious—drove the United States toward some sort of treaty with Japan. The only question was, as Senator William H. Seward of New York put it, "Why have not the United States before sent an expedition to the East?"

No doubt Seward knew that there had been previous expeditions to Japan, though not all of them had been sent by the government. The first American vessels to call there were probably the Boston sloop *Lady Washington* and the *Grace* of New York, which arrived in 1791 and tried to open up trade with southern Japan. In vain. All through the early 1800's Yankee captains continued to visit Japan. While their voyages contributed something to American knowledge of Japanese waters—knowledge that Commodore Perry was to call upon before setting out—no permanent ties of commerce or friendship were established.

Typical was the voyage of Charles W. King in the *Morrison* in 1837. Before leaving China, King had his brig's guns removed, and took aboard gifts for those Japanese officials who might welcome him. Being a shrewd Yankee trader, he also took along some American textiles, hoping that he might get a chance to sell or barter them. But his most important cargo—and his chief hope for a favorable reception—was a group of seven Japanese sailors, three of whom had been cast ashore on the American coast and four in China. Twice the *Morrison* sought to land, but each time shore batteries, hastily set up at word of her approach, drove her away. Finally she was forced to return to China, her gifts, trade goods, and Japanese sailors still aboard.

In 1844 the American whaler *Manhattan,* Captain Mercator Cooper, dropped anchor in lower Edo (Tokyo) Bay with another group of Japanese castaways. Just as he thought he was going to gain admittance to Edo, Cooper received a letter from the authorities. "The Emperor sends his compliments to me and thanks me for picking up their men," he later wrote, "and sends me word that i must not come again." The following morning a swarm of small boats surrounded the *Manhattan,* attached lines to her, and pulled her out to sea.

Naturally, humiliating experiences like these produced their echoes in the press and in Washington. As early as 1836, in fact, a sea captain named Edmund Roberts was dispatched by President Andrew Jackson with a letter to the Japanese emperor. Roberts died on the way, the letter undelivered. In 1846 Commodore James Biddle was assigned to transport to the emperor's court another would-be American commissioner, Alexander Everett; when Everett fell sick and had to leave the ship at Rio de Janeiro, Biddle forged ahead on his own, arriving in Edo Bay with the

Columbus and the *Vincennes* on July 20.

Here was no merchant skipper come to beg for trading privileges. This mission was in the hands of the United States Navy. Biddle announced at once that he was determined not to leave without a treaty, and he immediately wrote out his proposals. But upon boarding a Japanese patrol boat to receive the official reply, he was pushed by a Japanese guard. Biddle made no attempt to punish the offender, contenting himself with his hosts' promise that they would see to it. The mistake was fatal to his mission, for Biddle had committed the cardinal offense in the Orient: he had lost "face." The authorities shortly rejected his proposals for a treaty, and the *Columbus* and the *Vincennes*, like the hapless *Manhattan* before them, were towed out to sea. It was a lesson that would not be lost upon Matthew Perry.

Once more, in 1849, a ship of the U.S. Navy put into Japanese waters. The sloop of war *Preble*, Commander James Glynn, had come to demand the release of American sailors allegedly held prisoner by the Japanese. Glynn blustered and threatened and—apparently for that reason—he eventually got his way. Glynn's success, and the earlier humiliations, would be remembered by the stiff-backed man who stood upon the *Susquehanna*'s quarter-deck in July of 1853, watching his men respond smartly to general quarters.

In 1846 the Navy suffered a loss of prestige in the Pacific when Commodore James Biddle's ships, the Columbus *and the* Vincennes, *were towed out of Edo Bay by Japanese guard boats. Biddle had seemed eminently prepared to lead the mission—behind him were nearly a half-century of service and a fine combat record—yet in Japan he failed to meet the need for iron-fisted diplomacy.*

2

Mt. Fuji has long been venerated in Japan as a guardian of the empire; depicted in a rare print, the 12,389-foot peak stands its solitary watch over the approaches to Edo Bay.

COLLECTION OF TSUNEO TAMBA, Y-1

BEHIND THE CLOSED DOOR

"For the future, let none, so long as the sun illuminates the world, presume to sail to Japan, not even in the quality of Ambassadors, and this declaration is *never to be revoked* on pain of death." With this proclamation in 1638, the Japanese summarily closed the door to the empire.

It would remain closed until Perry's arrival in the summer of 1853. For 215 years no one would be allowed, according to the law, to enter or to leave Japan. To make sure that not a soul slipped out, edicts had been issued forbidding the building of ships big enough to survive in the open sea. Should a Japanese somehow succeed in getting out of the country, return meant death—the same penalty inflicted upon foreigners who sought to enter the kingdom.

The Japanese suspicion of foreigners was not groundless; it was based on a series of historic misunderstandings and tragedies. Once, a message had been intercepted which seemed to prove that the foreigners were plotting to take over Japan. It was easy to believe that the sacred traditions of the country were threatened by the probing, insistent men of the West.

Portuguese traders were the first Westerners to reach the islands, shortly before the sixteenth century. In the steps of the merchants came missionaries, and soon a Christian mission was established at Nagasaki. Thus it happened that early relations between Europe and Japan were more concerned with God than with trade.

The country at that time was emerging from a long period of civil war and was eager for contact with the outside world. In 1549 the Spanish-born Jesuit Francis Xavier, one of the greatest missionaries of all time, set out for Japan—three centuries before Perry appeared over the horizon. Xavier and his companions, having taken passage from Malaya in a Chinese pirate ship, landed and were welcomed at Kagoshima, near Nagasaki at the southwestern tip of the island chain.

The priests were given permission

to preach, and although Japan's language and customs were strange to them, they made conversions. By 1561 a Jesuit in Japan was writing to his superiors for help. "For the love of our Lord," he pleaded, "send us six or at least four of our Company, for not only in these [western provinces] but elsewhere the door is open for the gospel."

Soon thereafter Japan's greatest chieftain befriended the Jesuits. He

A familiar sight at Nagasaki in the early 1600's was the arrival of Portuguese merchant vessels carrying silks, gold, trinkets, and occasionally, Catholic missionaries. Here, Portuguese officers in pegged pantaloons are greeted by priests and a few high-ranking dignitaries.

"These are the best people so far discovered..." was the enthusiastic report of missionary Francis Xavier (left) after arriving in Japan in 1549. In the map below, made about thirty-five years later, cathedrals with flags indicate flourishing centers of Christianity within the empire.

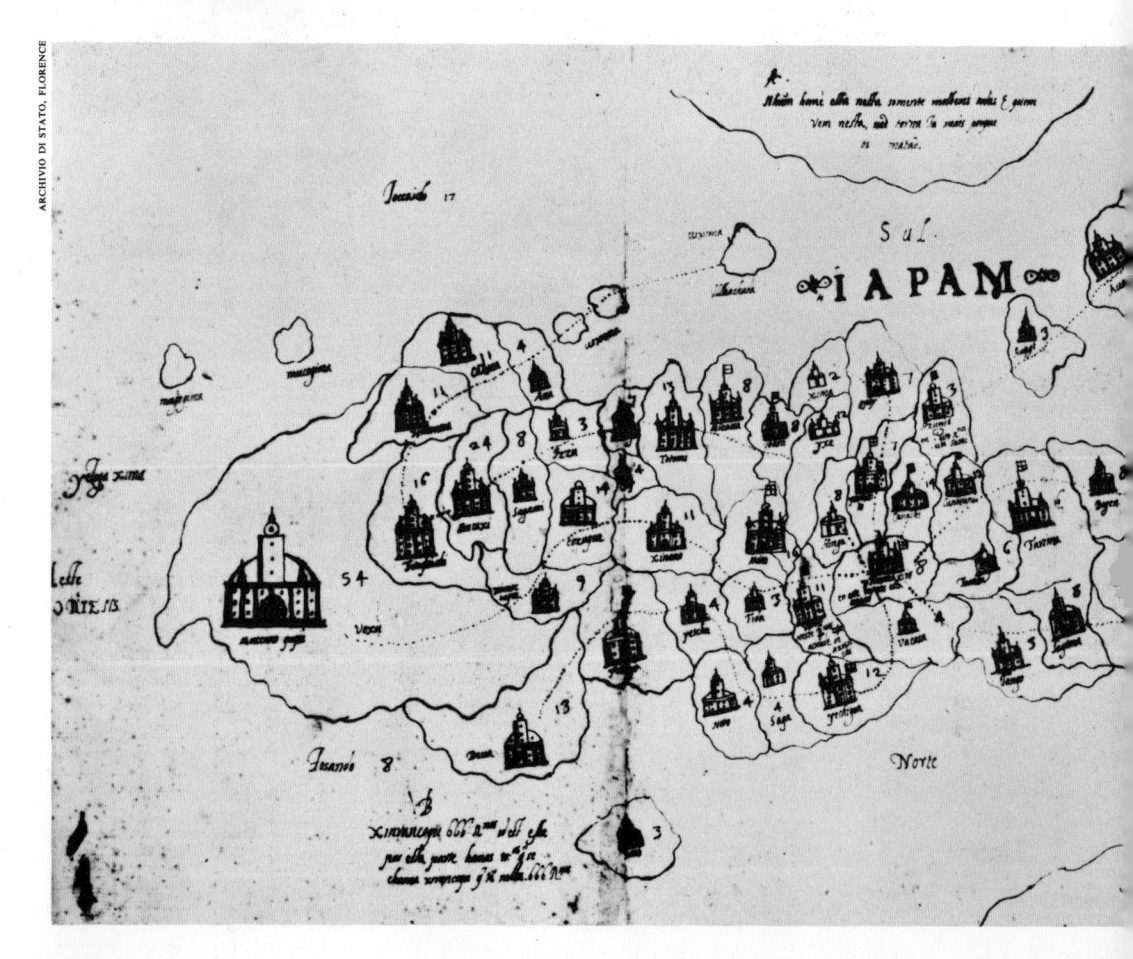

donated land for a seminary, and such was his influence that, as a modern historian has written, "It became almost fashionable in some quarters to be baptized and to carry a rosary, and many who had hesitated to take the last steps to conversion now came forward when they saw that Christianity had such high protection." The number of Christians, which had been a mere 1,500 in 1568, multiplied so rapidly that by 1582 there were 150,000. Most of them lived in the western provinces, but in Kyoto, the capital, there was a Christian community of 10,000 which included some of the most important men in Japan.

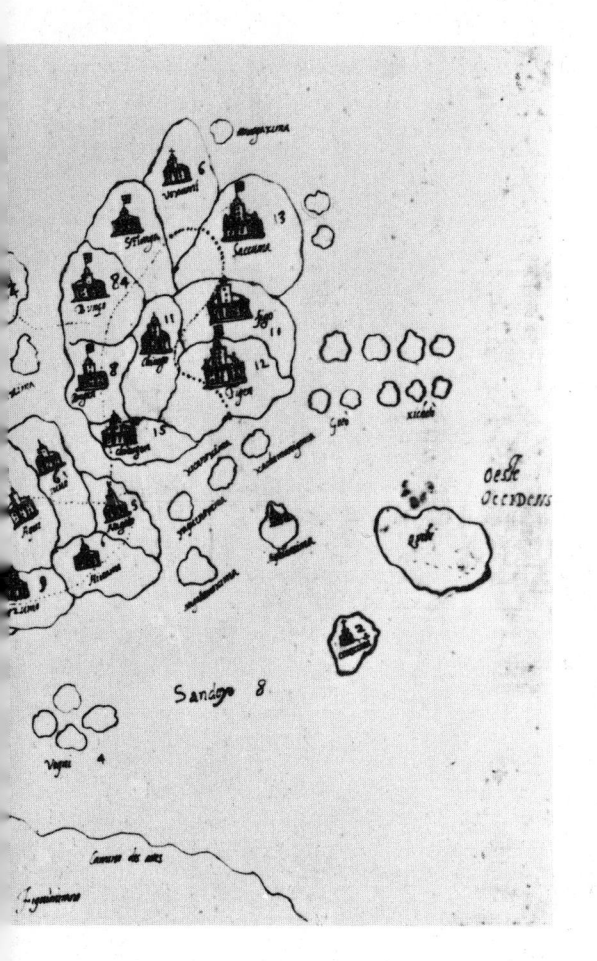

Then the chieftain died and his successor, a baron named Hideyoshi, suddenly decreed that the missionaries should leave Japan within twenty days. Hideyoshi had nothing against the priests or the doctrine they preached, but he felt they were undermining the empire.

There were substantial reasons for Hideyoshi's fears; in Japan, religion and government were very closely tied together. Historically, the emperor, or mikado, claimed to be divine—the living descendant of the sun god—and he stood at the peak of the social and political structure of the country. As the years and the decades rolled on, however, real power passed to the hands of a chief minister–or shogun as he was called—and the emperor was reduced to a ceremonial and religious figurehead.

Although, at the time of his edict against the Christians, the warlike Hideyoshi had more power than either the emperor or the shogun, he was determined that nothing would threaten the imperial regime. If the native religion of the country were supplanted by a foreign one, he was certain that the emperor's prestige would vanish and

OVERLEAF: *Tethered to stakes, twenty-two Christians await death by slow fire in the "great martyrdom" at Nagasaki in 1622. Another twenty-five were beheaded in this mass execution, a part of the anti-Catholic crusade that swept Japan at the time.*
CHIESA DEL GESU, ROME

MARTYRES LII.
IN IAPON. U X. SEPT.
MDCXXII

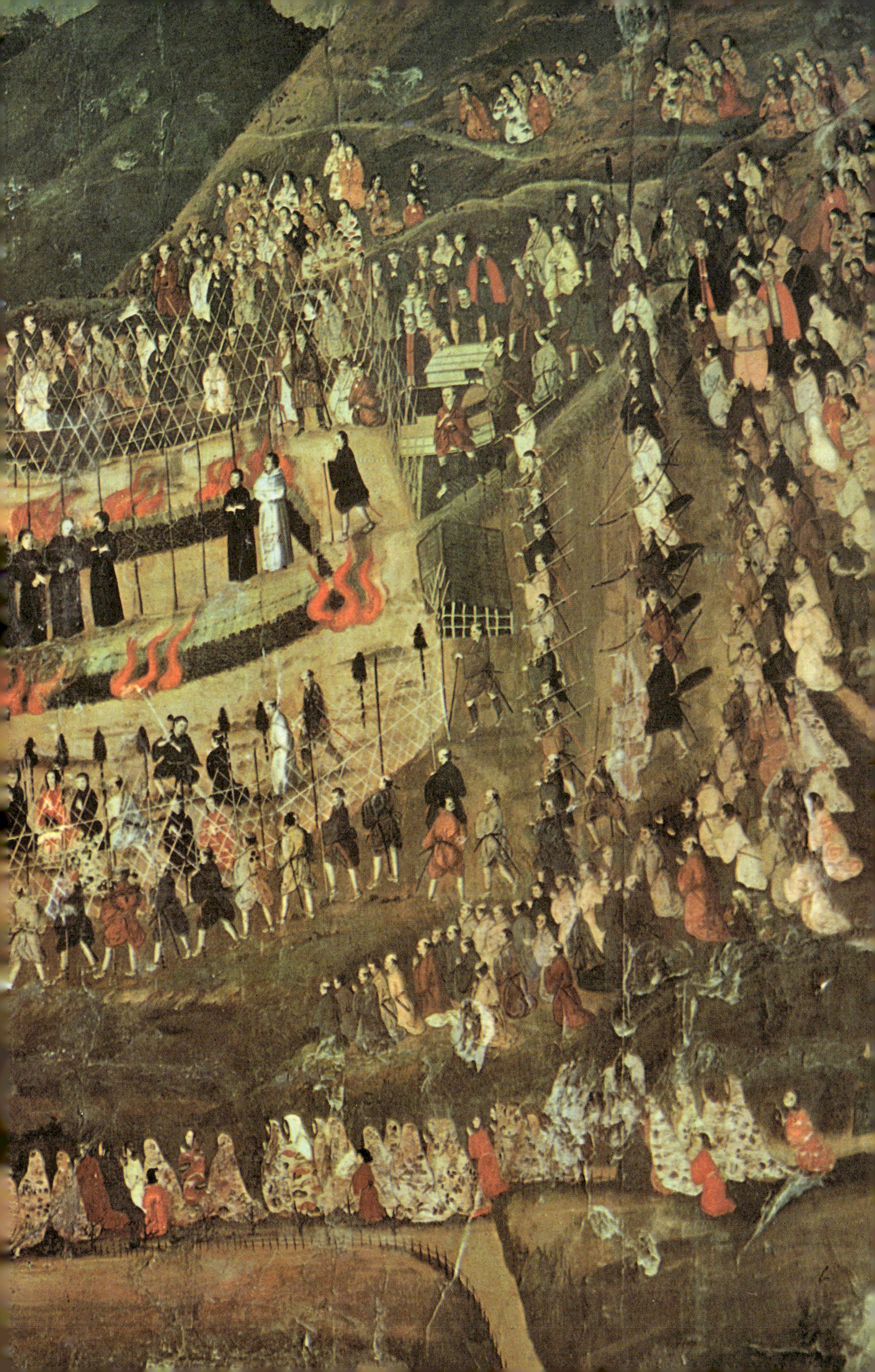

the whole structure of Japanese society would collapse with him. Thus, banishing the missionaries was a logical step for Hideyoshi, and not a demonstration of fanatical intolerance.

For ten years the expulsion decree was not strictly enforced, and the Jesuits were quietly tolerated so long as they acted with discretion. Then other Catholic missionaries arrived—the Franciscans—who, less cautious than the Jesuits, blatantly defied the decree by preaching openly. As the seventeenth century began, Christianity was again becoming a serious threat to the empire.

By then Hideyoshi had died, and national power had passed to Ieyasu Tokugawa, who re-established the authority of the shogun and ruled Japan in that role. In an effort to secure his political standing, he moved the capital from Kyoto to Edo (modern Tokyo) and ordered that Japan's Christian population be persecuted. Tens of thousands of Japanese converts were hunted down and executed. An English sea captain, hardly in sympathy with the Catholic church, was sickened by the slaughter. "There are many in prison," he wrote, "who hourly await death, for very few return to their idolatry." Those who did give up their faith to avoid death were required to repeat aloud a set formula. Part of it tells very clearly why the shoguns feared Christianity: "The fathers, by threats of excommunication and hell fire can do what they like with the people, and all this is their stratagem to take the countries of others."

To guard against such "stratagems," the Tokugawas put Japan under strict military dictatorship. The old feudal arrangement, whereby the country was divided into fiefs ruled over by daimyos supported by soldiers called samurai, was strengthened. A rigid class structure was set up, and the shoguns with their Council of Elders sought to regulate the smallest details of their subjects' lives. Even the kind of clothes each class could wear was determined by law.

But this was not enough. Still fearful of foreign influence, the Tokugawas after 1637 completed the expulsion of foreigners and closed Japan to the outside world. Only the Dutch, who had helped put down an uprising of Christian peasants in 1637, were permitted to stay, but their access was limited to a trading post on the tiny island of Deshima in the harbor of Nagasaki.

Once a year a Dutch envoy was accorded an audience at the shogun's palace, "The Hall of the Hundred Mats," at Edo. There he presented the gifts sent from Holland to the shogun and his council. During the nineteenth century an American businessman who had had many contacts with the Dutch described the humiliating audience: "After being compelled to make many degrading obeisances, to crawl on his hands and knees to a place shown him . . . then kneeling, [the Dutch envoy] bows his forehead

As "barbarian-expelling generalissimos," the Tokugawa shoguns ruled Japan for nearly 270 years. In the ceremony depicted here, the last shogun receives officials in an ornate chamber.

Commenting boldly that the emperor's court "surpasses even Solomon's throne in Splendor," Gleason's Pictorial, *an American newspaper, published this "elaborate picture" of the mikado giving an audience at his palace in 1853.*

to the ground, and retires, crawling backwards, without being permitted to look up or utter a single word. On some occasions, the envoy and his suite have been required to dance, sing, play on musical instruments, and practice buffoonery for the amusement of the seogoon [shogun] and his court."

For more than two hundred years —until Commodore Perry's arrival— all trade and communication with the world outside had to pass through the narrow funnel at Deshima. The relationship was such, the American businessman disgustedly pointed out, as to inspire the Japanese rulers "with a profound contempt for foreigners of the Western nations."

But there were cracks in the wall that had been built between Japan and the Western world. For one thing, especially after 1720, when foreign books (providing they did not deal with Christianity) were permitted entry through Deshima, Japanese students began to develop a thirst for Western knowledge. They asked the

Dutch traders to teach them their language, and along with the rules of grammar, the traders succeeded in imparting something of the political, scientific, and artistic affairs of the outside world.

As Perry was to learn, the Japanese were not entirely uninformed about America. In 1644 the shoguns asked the Dutch at Deshima to send them an annual report, a kind of roundup of world news. Each year when the shipment of goods arrived from Holland, the *opperhoofd*, the director of the trading post, would question the officers of the vessel, scan whatever newspapers or books they happened to have aboard, write up his report, and submit it to Edo through the local officials at Nagasaki. The reports continued, and after 1745 they began to include information about Britain's colonies in North America. Between 1790 and 1807 news of the outside world probably increased. The Dutch during those years were engaged in wars with other European nations, and began to hire American ships to take their goods to Japan.

Information obtained by Japanese interpreters through the *opperhoofd* in 1809, for instance, included a fairly accurate account of the American Revolution and the establishment of the United States: "About the year 1775 or 1776, the people of North America raised troops and fought in revolt against England, because the English oppressed them and exacted taxes from them. The fighting con-

A delegation of feudal lords (seated in sedan chairs) and their samurai retainers put on an impressive display of pomp as they prepare to enter the shogun's walled palace at Edo.

tinued until . . . the English were finally driven out . . . and an independent nation was established. . . . In every state, in North America today, a unified government has been established, and chiefs set up, among whom one called Jefferson is particularly famous." "Chief" Thomas Jefferson was, in fact, just finishing his second term as President of the United States.

An eyewitness account of the New World was added to secondhand reports when in 1843 a young Japanese saw America for himself. He was a poor fisherman named Manjiro, who at the age of fourteen started out with four others on a routine fishing trip. Blown out to sea by a storm, their small boat was cast up on an uninhabited North Pacific island. After living there for five months, subsisting on seaweed, fish, and rain water, they were rescued by the American whaler *John Howland* under the command of Captain William H. Whitfield of Fairhaven, Massachusetts.

The whaler was heading for Honolulu, and on the way Manjiro, by his cheerfulness and willingness to work, so endeared himself to the widowed and childless Whitfield that he became almost like a son. Manjiro, whose own father was dead, returned the affection. When they reached Hawaii, the captain offered Manjiro his choice of waiting there for a ship that might take him back toward Japan, or going to America on the *John Howland*. The boy, whom Whit-

METROPOLITAN MUSEUM OF ART, ROGERS FUND, 1904

Wrought from iron and leather, the elaborate suit of armor at left dates from about 1550 and was worn by a samurai officer in the service of one of Japan's great princes. The samurai warriors grouped above were painted at the time of Perry's visit. Although their class had become powerless, they could manage warlike poses; their armor, like that opposite, was obsolete, and their weapons inadequate.

field had nicknamed "John Mung" because the sailors could not pronounce his Japanese name, decided he would like to see the United States. His four companions remained in Hawaii.

On May 7, 1843, the *Howland* dropped anchor at its home port of New Bedford, Massachusetts. Soon afterward Captain Whitfield married again and took the boy to live with him and his bride. It was to be seven years—during which John Mung would grow from a boy to a man—before he returned to Japan.

Those years were full of adventure. Just being in a strange country—going to school, learning a new language, observing the customs and dress of the people around him—was a revelation to Manjiro. He was a bright boy, and after a short time in the village school, he enrolled in special classes to learn mathematics and the fundamentals of navigation. In 1845 an opportunity came to use his new skills, on a whaling cruise aboard the ship *Franklin*. Manjiro—he was nineteen now—signed on. The *Franklin* went all the way to the Pacific Ocean, and in the course of the long voyage the captain became insane. The first mate assumed command, and so popular was Manjiro with his shipmates that they unanimously elected him second officer.

When they returned to New Bedford in 1849, the men of the *Franklin* learned that gold had just been discovered in California. Why not, Man-

Dutch and Chinese ships, foreign merchants, and the trading island of Deshima (above, at right center) can be found in this seventeenth-century map of Nagasaki's landlocked harbor. By inverting many details, the cartographer hoped to maintain artistic perspective.

For two hundred years the tiny post of Deshima, barely a third of a mile long and a fifth of a mile wide, was the only Western foothold in Japan; its one connection with the mainland was a heavily guarded bridge (above). At right, Dutch and Japanese merchants weigh a shipment of goods bound for Europe.

jiro thought, seek his fortune in the gold fields? Besides, despite the risk, he wanted to return to his aging mother in Japan. Once in California, he would be halfway home.

He worked his way around Cape Horn on a lumber ship and in May of 1850 arrived in the booming town of San Francisco. He went prospecting, and one day discovered a nugget of gold almost as big as an egg. He decided to sell it and, with this money and his share of the profits from the whaling voyage, buy passage to Japan. At Honolulu he transferred to another ship, the *Sarah Boyd*, bound for China to pick up a cargo of tea. Before leaving Hawaii, Manjiro persuaded two of the fishermen with whom he had been shipwrecked to go back home with him. (One of the four had died in the meantime, and the other preferred to stay in Honolulu.)

Knowing that the *Sarah Boyd* would never be permitted to land in Japan, they bought a small boat and took it on board with them. When they neared their home waters, they asked the captain to put their boat into the sea; they would go on alone.

The captain, aware of the dangers that lay ahead of them, tried to persuade the three Japanese not to go. Manjiro would not be swayed. "If I don't take this chance, I may never see my mother," he is reported to have said. "Besides, I must return to my countrymen at once and tell them that they must open their eyes before it is too late. They cannot remain isolated from the rest of the world forever."

Manjiro and his shipmates landed on Okinawa, one of the Ryukyu Islands—a Japanese dependency nearly 350 miles southwest of the mainland. Here they were held prisoners for seven months before being taken to Japan. Suspicion of Christianity had not vanished; at Nagasaki they had to pass the test then required of anyone suspected of Christian sympathies—they had to trample on the *fumie*, a small brass image of Jesus crucified. Officials examined Manjiro no less than eighteen times, not only to make sure he was loyal to the homeland, but also to get information about the countries he had visited. Manjiro was able to tell them a good deal and bring them up to date on the Presidency. In America, he told his interrogators, "a man of great knowledge and ability is elected king who holds his office for four years and then he is succeeded by another." This august individual "lives a very simple life and goes out on horseback accompanied by one servant," Manjiro continued. The current "king" was Zachary Taylor, a hero of the recent war between the United States and Mexico.

At last Manjiro was freed and allowed to return to his mother, with whom he was reunited amid tears of joy. Once a poor fisherman with no prospects of ever being anything more, he was now an honored personage who had seen the world and its wonders. Within the week he was taken into the service of the shogun.

The government Manjiro entered in that winter of 1851 was in dire straits. Almost every class within Japan was dissatisfied. The long period of the Tokugawa dictatorship had, it was true, been a period of peace. But this had proved a mixed blessing. The power of the shogun rested upon daimyos, or feudal barons, who in turn were dependent upon samurai, the warriors of Japan. In peacetime, the samurai were not needed, and so their pay was reduced. The samurai grumbled.

Near the end of the eighteenth century a Japanese had scornfully described another fact that told of the decline of the samurai. "If on taking a test they are lucky enough to hit a two-foot target and to dismount safely after bestriding a horse as tame as a cat, they are promoted for their exploits and after that they put their accomplishments on the shelf." The martial talents of these once-proud warriors were rusting from disuse.

Also, the farmers were rebellious. A dictatorship has to be supported by someone. In Japan it was supported for the most part by a heavy tax on rice. Not only was this the peasant's principal food, it was also the only thing he had to sell, the only way he could raise money. If the rice crop failed, he was in trouble. And

Socializing at Deshima, these Japanese seem completely at home with their Dutch hosts; yet they could have been dealt stiff penalties for mingling with the outcast Westerners.

ボーシトン
府馬頭
之菌

高サ四百尺ニ九百尺ニ盈
名ヲチ、フトト呼

絶末船ノ形チヲ造リ
其輪轉ヲ見テ以テ風
位ヲ知ル

中間ニ巨大ノ
時計ヲ設ク假
令望山ノ遠モ能
分明ナラシム

from about 1700 on, the crop did fail all too often. Severe famines resulted in frequent "rice riots," aimed not so much at overthrowing the regime as at securing some tax relief.

Japanese merchants and bankers in the towns were as dissatisfied as the samurai and the people of the countryside. The Tokugawa government seems never to have been able to manage the kingdom's finances efficiently. The shogun and his daimyos were constantly borrowing from the businessmen; when they could not pay their debts, they simply canceled them. The businessmen went bankrupt. And finally, from the scholars and intellectuals of Japan the clamor increased for more contacts with the West.

Thus, at the start of the nineteenth century, there was a strong current of discontent within the mysterious kingdom. The Japanese yearned for a change. Pressures from within the country were strong—strong enough, perhaps, that they might have opened Japan to the West even had there been no pressures from without. But there were; foreign ships appeared on the horizon, and not only from the United States.

In the half-century before Perry's arrival, at least three Russian expeditions had approached Japan—in 1792, 1804, and 1811. A British man-of-war put into Nagasaki in 1808 to demand water and provisions, and over the next forty years four other British ships approached the islands

Among Manjiro's indelible impressions of his journey to America, two stand out: his rescue by the John Howland *(above) and Boston's Old North Church (left). Years later, Manjiro was to participate in Japan's negotiations with Perry and in his nation's first diplomatic mission to the U. S.*
BOTH: COLLECTION OF EMILY V. WARINNER

OVERLEAF: *"She runs as quick as a dragon in swimming," wrote a Japanese after watching the performance of an American steamship in 1853. An artist, obviously awed by the clouds of black smoke and the monkey-like agility of the crewmen, combined imagination with accuracy in drawing this view.*
COLLECTION OF CARL H. BOEHRINGER

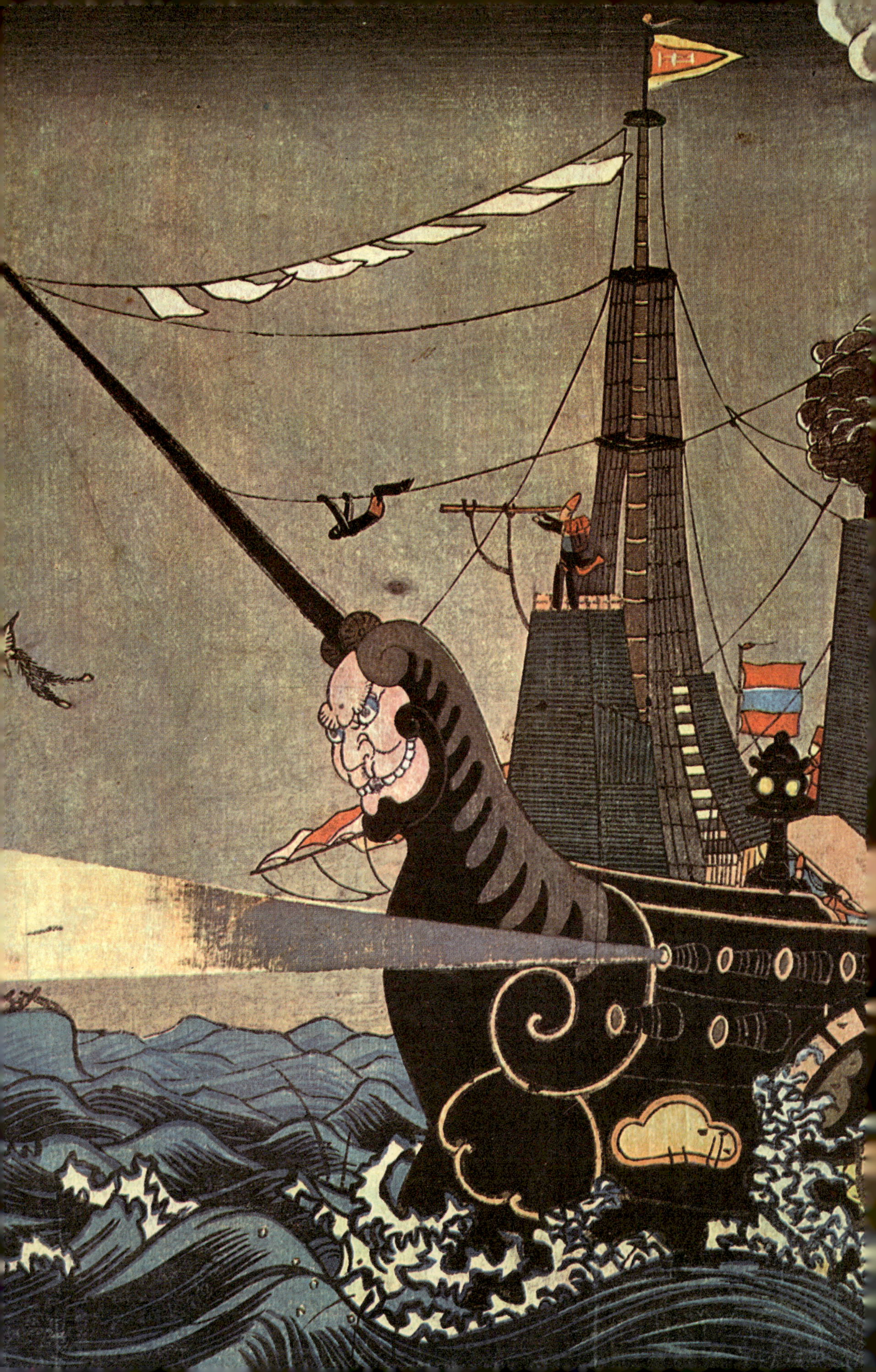

長サ七十五間
船巾二十間
車六間半
帆柱三本
水ヨリ上ノ出貳丈五尺
石火矢二十挺
大筒貳十五挺

for trade and surveying. A French admiral called there in 1846.

None of these visitors had conquest in mind; none had the perseverance or the degree of backing from his government that Perry would have. But the Japanese authorities thought they did. Frightened, the shogun in 1825 issued a decree known as the *Ni-nen-naku*, or "No Second Thought," order. Local officials were commanded to destroy, on sight, any foreign ship that sought to anchor, and to arrest or kill any sailors who came ashore. It was this order that had caused Charles W. King in the *Morrison* to be fired upon in 1837.

The *Morrison* affair caused a good deal of criticism inside Japan. Obviously, it would make a bad impression on foreigners, and after the so-called Opium War of 1839–42, in which a strong British fleet had soundly trounced the Chinese, Japanese authorities had a healthy respect for foreign navies. In 1842, therefore, the "No Second Thought" order was relaxed. Local officials were now told that if Western ships approached, they should be given water and provisions and advised to leave. This was probably the real reason why neither Captain Cooper in the *Manhattan,* James Biddle commanding the *Vincennes* and *Columbus,* nor Commander Glynn in the *Preble* had been greeted by gunfire.

It was apparent that the shogun and his council did not know what to do. Two hundred years of tradition told them to keep the door closed—but pressures, from within and without, were forcing it open. Not long after Manjiro's return, Commodore Perry was receiving orders that would send him on the long voyage to Japan and compel its rulers to make up their minds.

By various means Japanese scholars were able to piece together accounts of political and cultural developments in the outside world. Scenes from a book published in 1853—just two years after Manjiro's return from America—show "Koronbus" and Queen "Isaberla" (opposite), and oddly, a confrontation between George Washington and sixteenth-century Italian explorer Amerigo Vespucci (above).

3

A New York newspaper celebrated Perry's departure for Japan with this drawing of the Commodore being rowed out to assume command of the Mississippi *(right foreground).*

OLD MATT TAKES COMMAND

J. WELLES HENDERSON, PHILADELPHIA MARITIME MUSEUM

In the course of his forty-four-year career in the Navy, Commodore Perry had acquired a reputation for leadership; the New York *Courier and Enquirer* called him "the most distinguished and proverbially the most efficient officer in the Navy." No one was surprised that he was selected to command the expedition to Japan.

Early he had been an outspoken advocate of rigid training and imaginative engineering. When the Naval Academy at Annapolis was established in 1845, he was one of five officers named to its administrative board. And when it became apparent that the days of sail were numbered, he was put in charge of building what would become the most famous ship of her time—the steamer *Mississippi*. During the Mexican War, the *Mississippi* was his flagship in his moment of triumph, the taking of Veracruz. Now, this stalwart ship was to carry him to the East.

In November of 1852, after seemingly endless delays, all was ready for Perry's departure—or as ready as it ever would be.

He had set about preparing for the expedition nine months before, when he had formally received his orders in Washington. Ships, of course, had been his first consideration. The Navy Department promised him an impressive fleet. He was to fly his flag from the masthead of the reliable old *Mississippi*. Just one other ship, the *Princeton,* a newer propeller-driven steamer, was to sail with him on the eastward voyage to the Pacific. Once having arrived in China, he was to be joined by the steamer *Susquehanna*, the sloops *Plymouth* and *Saratoga*, and the storeship *Supply.* To these would be added, "at the earliest day practicable," the *Vermont,* a 74-gun ship of the line not yet out of the builder's yard, as well as the steamer *Alleghany,* the sloop *Vandalia,* the corvette *Macedonian,* and a second storeship, the *Southampton.* Altogether, Perry would have eleven ships. It would be a formidable squadron.

To command it, Perry selected the best officers he could get. Many had served under him in Mexico. Others, like Flag Lieutenant Silas Bent, Glynn's navigator on the *Preble* in 1849, were selected because they knew something about Japan. Still others were men whom Perry personally knew to be reliable officers who shared his way of doing things. Fifty-two-year-old Franklin Buchanan was made captain of the fleet; one of the Commodore's staunchest backers in the effort to train a professional officer class, Buchanan had been the first commandant of the Naval Academy.

As for the junior officers, Buchanan was instructed to choose men "of a subordinate and gentleman-like character," for flogging had been recently abolished in the Navy, and on this trip, Perry pointed out, the crews would have to be governed "by moral suasion." Apparently Buchanan was under some pressure in making up his rosters, for as news of the approaching voyage spread, he was besieged by applications to join the expedition. Reporters clamored to cover the trip, sailors wanted to be a part of the prestigious undertaking, and many wealthy families sought to have their sons join this great—and presumably educational—adventure. Two who were accepted were the eighteen-year-old Lewis twins, John and Lawrence, great-grandnephews of George Washington.

But raw recruits or experienced sailors, the men on the expedition feared and respected Perry. They were close enough to him to see not the myth which the fifty-eight-year-old Commodore had become but the man himself. "He was bluff, positive and stern on duty, and a terror to the ignorant and lazy. But the faithful ones who performed their duties . . . held him in the highest estimation." So wrote a subordinate of the heavily built, immaculately dressed man known throughout the Navy as "Old Matt."

In only one case did Perry permit favoritism to influence his choice of

U.S. NAVAL ACADEMY MUSEUM

Before carrying him to the distant Orient, the reliable steamer Mississippi *saw service with the Commodore in the Mexican War. The 1847 drawing above, by an American officer, shows the powerful warship heading Perry's six-mile-long squadron as it ascends Mexico's Tabasco River.*

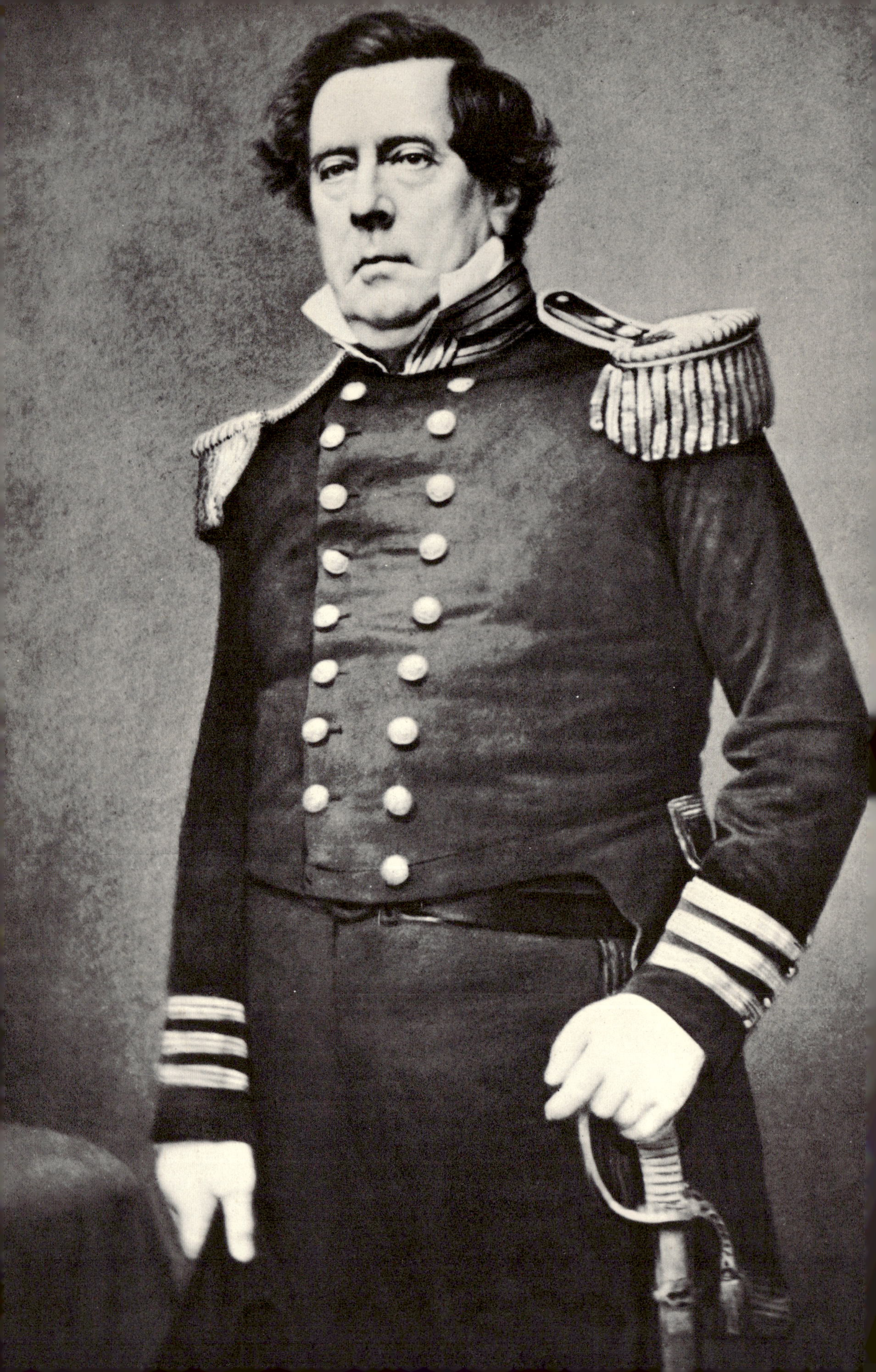

Oliver Hazard Perry (right), portrayed at the height of his career by Rembrandt Peale, looks every bit the dashing, romantic hero he was in life. Despite their physical differences, Oliver had much in common with his stern younger brother, Matthew Calbraith, photographed at left. Both men were strong-willed and daring, and both displayed a great flair for the dramatic.

personnel. To serve as his clerk on the expedition, he appointed his son, Lieutenant Oliver Hazard Perry, namesake of the Commodore's famous older brother, who had so brilliantly defeated the British in the Battle of Lake Erie during the War of 1812. But Old Matt saw to it that this appointment would not be used against him. To avoid public criticism, he sent young Oliver ahead to China on a commercial passenger ship, paying the fare himself. There, far from the public eye, the boy could be taken aboard the flagship, and no one would be the wiser.

Ships and men selected, Perry turned his thoughts to the details of charts and coal for his four steamers. He got in touch with the firm of Howland & Aspinwall of New York and instructed them to send coal ahead to ports where he thought he would not be able to buy it—to Capetown, South Africa, and to the island of Mauritius, in the Indian Ocean. The charts—$30,000 worth—he obtained from the Dutch, who remained the only Westerners with up-to-date knowledge of Japan.

Evidence seems to suggest that the Commodore himself had a long-abiding interest in the Orient. He owned many books on the subject, and now he bought more. For other information he traveled to New Bedford, home port of many American whalers (including the *John Howland*, which had rescued Manjiro); there he talked with captains and mates who knew the winds and weather and the channels and currents near the Japanese islands.

It is customary on any diplomatic mission to bring gifts for one's hosts. Since one of his main objectives was to establish regular trade arrangements with Japan, Commodore Perry set out to assemble a representative

53

array of American products that would impress the Japanese and make them eager to become paying customers. Manufacturers were happy to donate samples of their wares. A complete telegraph outfit was given to Perry, and the arms maker Samuel Colt sent along $1,000 worth of his latest pistols, rifles, and ammunition. From Norris & Brothers of Philadelphia came a quarter-size steam train—engine, tender, one car, and 370 feet of track. It was to be the hit of Perry's expedition.

Then there was the last-minute business of Perry's official orders— who had sufficient strategic knowledge to write them? Secretary of State Webster decreed that the Commodore himself was the "proper person to draft his instructions," and promptly ordered him to do so.

Consequently, Perry directed himself to obtain a treaty that would guarantee protection for American sailors shipwrecked off Japan; permit American ships to put into Japanese harbors for supplies; set up coaling stations in the islands; provide for the opening of ports for trade; and begin the regular exchange of consuls between the two nations. A letter from President Millard Fillmore, embodying most of these demands and beginning, "Great and Good Friend," was aboard the flagship to be delivered to the mikado.

Finally, on November 17, 1852, the last stores were piled on the *Mississippi*'s decks. The two-ship expedition got under way; but almost immediately the *Princeton*, always a hardluck ship, broke down. The *Mississippi* went on alone. Black smoke pouring from her funnel, her paddlewheels churning the water, she left Chesapeake Bay behind, dropped her pilot, and set her course across the Atlantic.

After touching at Madeira and at the Canaries off the northwest shoulder of Africa, the *Mississippi* headed south and east for Capetown, stopping briefly at British-owned St. Helena, where the crew visited the original tomb of Napoleon. From Capetown she headed around the Cape of Good Hope and into the Indian Ocean. Pausing at Mauritius and Ceylon, she threaded her way through the Straits of Malacca, touched at Singapore, and crossed the South China Sea to anchor at last at Hong Kong. It was April 6, 1853. She had been on the way nearly four and a half months.

As she steamed into port, the *Mississippi* was saluted by the *Plymouth*, the *Saratoga*, and the storeship *Supply*, which had been waiting for her. But the ship Perry was really looking for—Buchanan's powerful steam frigate *Susquehanna*—was nowhere in sight. There was a civil war going on in China, and American merchants along the coast had pressured their diplomatic officials into demanding that the Navy use the warship for their protection.

There was nothing for it but to fol-

In the 1830's, as commander of the Brooklyn Navy Yard (above), Perry had a formidable reputation. On meeting the Commodore, a sailor wrote, "Matt looked at me from stem to stern. His gaze I thought he ne'er would turn...."

low the *Susquehanna* to Shanghai and join forces there. Along the way, in Macao, the Commodore picked up his son. "Oliver is on board," he wrote his wife, "and has commenced his new duties." At Canton he took on another passenger, Dr. Samuel Wells Williams, who spoke Japanese and had been aboard the *Morrison* on her voyage to Japan in 1837. Apparently this talented American missionary and linguist, whom Perry from the first had wanted for his interpreter, was not quite so anxious to leave Canton as Old Matt had hoped. But Perry was persuasive; he planned, he said, to have a spacious cabin built for Williams on the deck of the *Susquehanna*, to which he intended to transfer his command pennant. He promised the missionary he would not have to work on the Sabbath, and assured him, perhaps with more confidence than he really felt, that there would be no fighting with the Japanese. "Wells went with Commodore

55

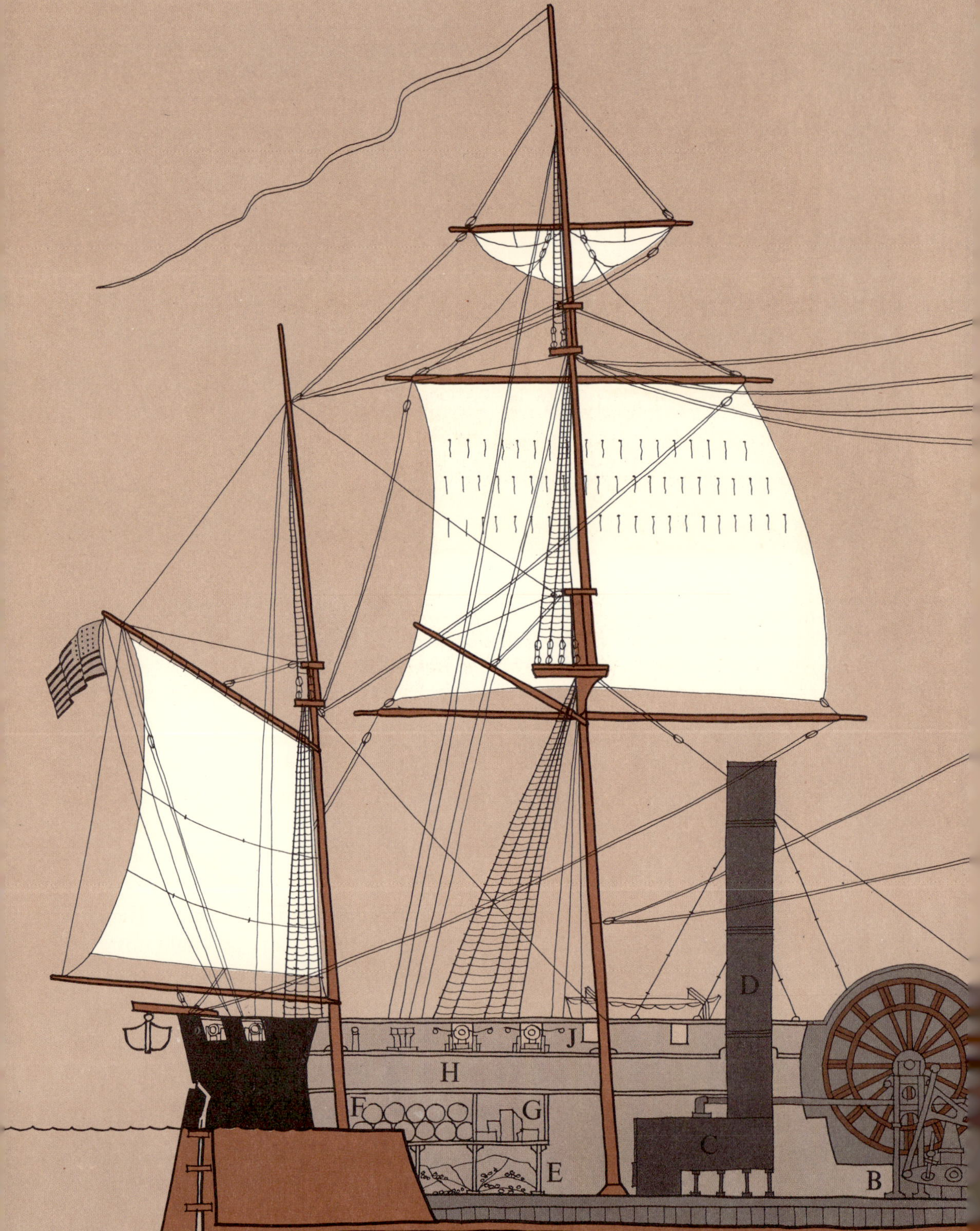
D
J
H
F
G
C
E
B

THE U.S.S. MISSISSIPPI

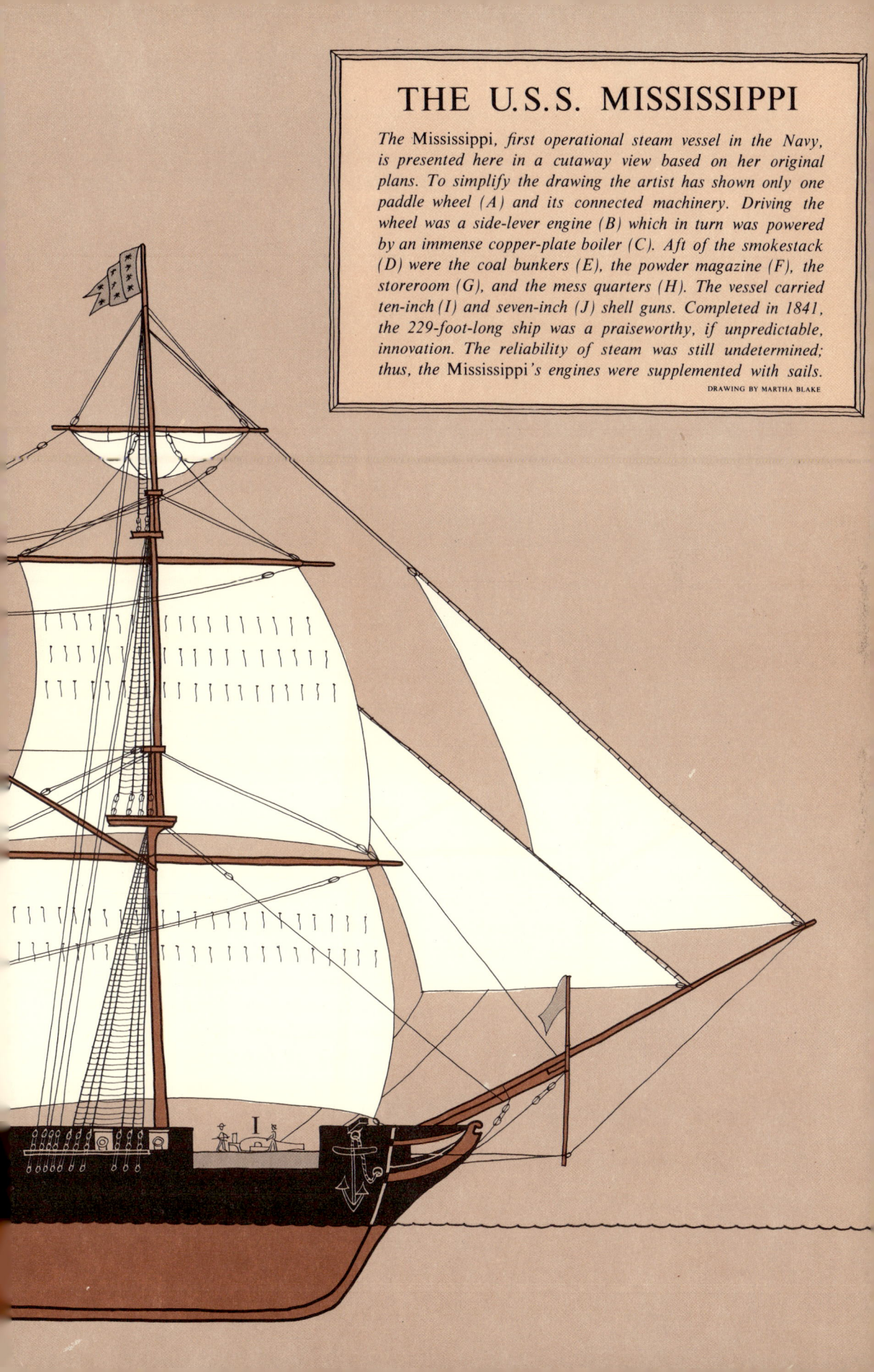

The Mississippi, *first operational steam vessel in the Navy, is presented here in a cutaway view based on her original plans. To simplify the drawing the artist has shown only one paddle wheel (A) and its connected machinery. Driving the wheel was a side-lever engine (B) which in turn was powered by an immense copper-plate boiler (C). Aft of the smokestack (D) were the coal bunkers (E), the powder magazine (F), the storeroom (G), and the mess quarters (H). The vessel carried ten-inch (I) and seven-inch (J) shell guns. Completed in 1841, the 229-foot-long ship was a praiseworthy, if unpredictable, innovation. The reliability of steam was still undetermined; thus, the* Mississippi's *engines were supplemented with sails.*

DRAWING BY MARTHA BLAKE

Perry," Mrs. Williams later wrote, "rather against his own (and much against *my*) will. . . ." But he went.

It was obvious to Perry that not all of the ships promised him would be available in the immediate future. He therefore planned two trips to Japan. In the spring of 1853, he would deliver President Fillmore's letter. The next year, having assembled a larger force, he would return for an answer and, if possible, negotiate a treaty.

He would stop first at the Ryukyu, or Loochoo, Islands—Perry called them the "Lew Chews." They would serve as a stopover base between the two voyages. Moreover, since they were a dependency of Japan, Perry might get some hint there of how he would be received on the mainland.

Reluctantly agreeing to leave the *Plymouth* at Shanghai to protect American business interests, the Commodore departed on the *Susquehanna* on May 23. After three days, with the sloop *Saratoga*, the little *Supply*, and the *Mississippi*, Perry sailed through a driving rain into the harbor of Naha, principal port of Okinawa, the largest island of the Ryukyus.

"The shores of the island were green and beautiful from the water," one of Perry's officers wrote, "diversified with groves and fields of the freshest verdure. The rain had brightened the colors of the landscape, which recalled to my mind the richest English scenery." Steep hills, covered with gardens and waving grain, sloped upward from the beaches, and at the head of the bay was Naha itself, its narrow streets paved with crushed coral, its low houses roofed with tile and walled about with stone.

Through their telescopes Perry and

Wilhelm Heine, the expedition's official artist, drew this scene of the American procession leaving the regent's palace near the port of Naha. Visible at left is the Commodore, enthroned in his Navy-styled sedan chair.

his officers could see curious crowds gathering along the water front, and within a short time a small boat, bearing two native officials, put out to the flagship. In the *Narrative* of the expedition, published in 1856 under his direction, the Commodore inserted a careful description of the encounter: "The principal personage wore a

59

loose salmon-colored robe of very fine grass cloth, while the dress of the other was of similar fashion, but of a blue color. On their heads were oblong caps of bright yellow. They had blue sashes around their waists and white sandals upon their feet. Their beards were long and black, though thin, and their ages were, seemingly, some thirty-five or forty years. They had the Japanese cast of countenance, and in complexion were a dusky olive."

When they climbed aboard and presented their calling card—a yard-long piece of red paper inscribed with Japanese characters—Perry refused to see them. This was not because of an inflated sense of his own dignity. Rather it was part of a carefully-thought-out plan. Old Matt thoroughly understood the importance the Oriental mind attached to rank. He had determined that both here and in Japan itself he would never deal with anyone of a status inferior to his own—and that, since he represented the President of the United States, meant the highest official to be found. The next morning, when the "Lew Chewans" sent fresh meat, vegetables, and eggs out to the ships, the Commodore refused to accept them. He would not be placed under any obligation to his hosts and thus give them an advantage in future negotiations.

A day later two American officers went ashore to explain to the local officials why Perry had not received them or their gifts, stating that the

PERRY'S VOYAGE TO JAPAN, 1853

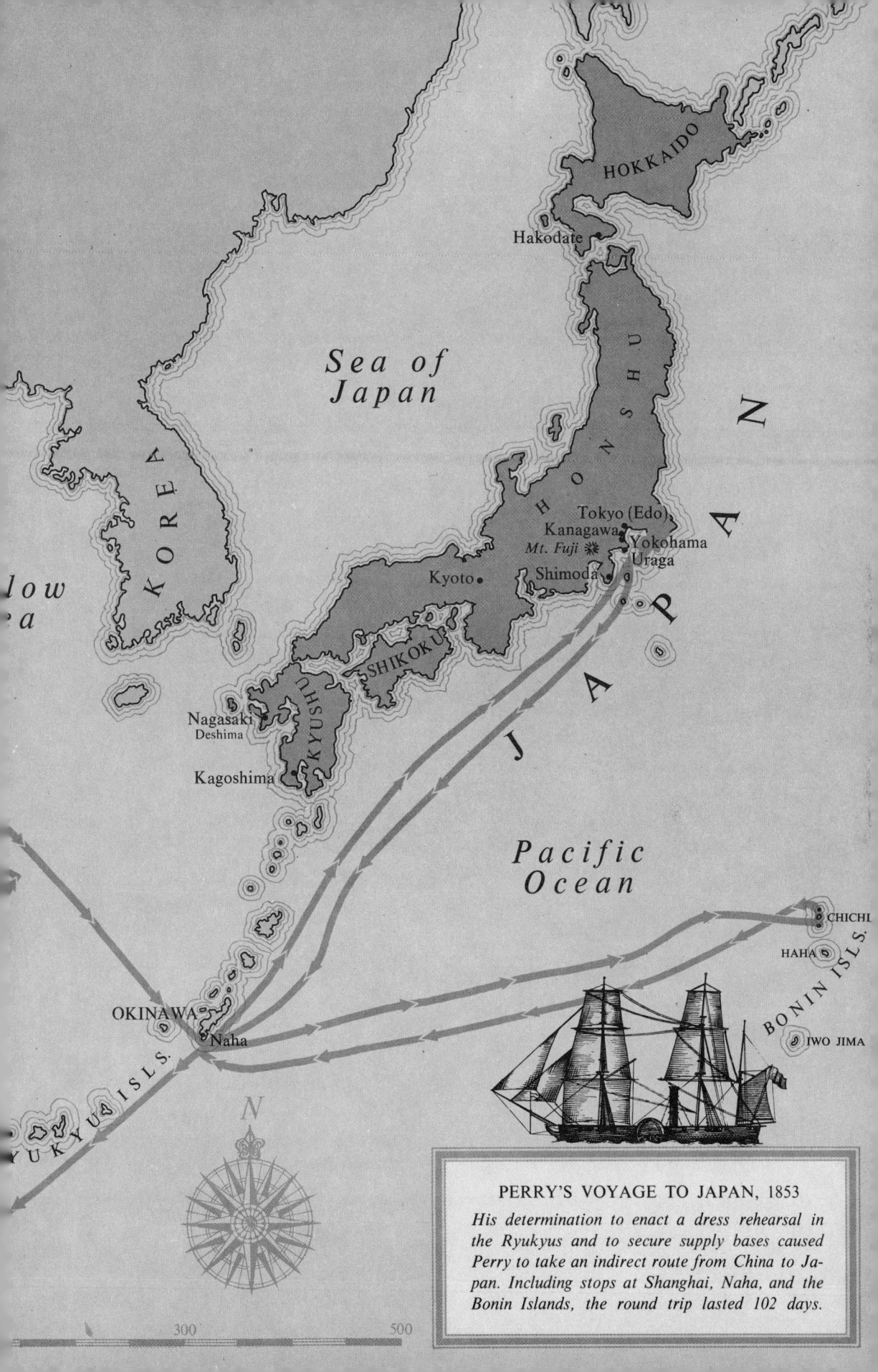

His determination to enact a dress rehearsal in the Ryukyus and to secure supply bases caused Perry to take an indirect route from China to Japan. Including stops at Shanghai, Naha, and the Bonin Islands, the round trip lasted 102 days.

Fearing Japanese criticism, the aged regent of Ryukyu, flanked by attendants in this contemporary print, did his wily best to prevent Perry from entering the sacred precincts of the royal palace.

Commodore would entertain personally only their highest official—who was, the officers learned, an elderly regent ruling in the name of an eleven-year-old prince. Perry was sure that this diplomatic chess game would affect his chances of success in Japan. The next move was up to the regent.

Meanwhile Perry would not let his men "eat the bread of idleness." He ordered a surveying party, with tents and supplies, to go ashore to map the island and estimate its natural resources. Two other surveying parties went by sea, one to circle the island to the east, the other to the west. Small boats put out from the steamers and sloops to chart Naha harbor, and when they had nothing else to do, the sailors were put through boat drills while the marines went through their paces on the beach.

On May 30 the regent finally took the bait and, accompanied by a party of about twenty, came out to the *Susquehanna* to meet Perry. The regent was a very old man, so feeble he had to be supported by two of his aides. The delegation was shown a number of American gadgets. A mirror made the regent's companions giggle, and feel behind the glass to see how it made a reflection. The tick-tick of a watch they imitated with their mouths; a glimpse of its works brought forth exclamations of surprise. The visitors were also shown around the ship, and when the engineer made the great pistons of the engine move, two or three of the visitors darted up the companionway, fearful that their lives were in danger.

Perry remained secluded in his cabin all this time. Only after the guests had been sufficiently impressed did he deign to receive them. It was a cordial meeting that lasted an hour and a half and ended with Perry's announcement that he intended to return the visit at the royal palace on the sixth of June—a week hence. He would expect, he said, to be received with all the ceremony due his rank and his position as the official representative of the United States.

This evidently produced a panic among the islanders. It was bad enough to have Perry's sailors, marines, and surveying parties roaming the island, but that foreigners should invade the royal palace—that was outrageous.

The regent and his aides tried every device they could think of to dissuade the Commodore. First they invited him to a great feast given by the mayor of Naha; since the regent would preside, Perry would thereupon be considered to have returned the visit. The Commodore recognized this as a shoddy substitute for the proper reception. He could not possibly attend the dinner, he replied; on the day appointed he planned to dispatch a supply ship to Shanghai, and that would demand all of his attention. Next his hosts begged him not to go to the royal palace, residence of the ailing queen dowager, but to visit that of the young prince instead. Perry, refusing to believe that the queen was ill—and half suspecting that she did not even exist—held firm. The pageantry of the reception and the music of his ships' bands would do her good, he observed piously; and he would bring along his ships' doctors to prescribe for her if she wished.

Promptly at 9 A.M. on June 6 the Commodore, accompanied by an impressive assemblage of officers, bandsmen, and marines, landed at Naha, and the procession to the palace formed up. Perry himself traveled in a large sedan chair hastily constructed by one of his carpenters and borne by four Chinese coolies, with four more standing by to relieve them. The chair was, in the words of the *Narrative*, "deeply indebted to paint and putty," and its red and blue hangings were less than elegant, but the natives were impressed. They formed three deep along the roadside as the Americans passed, those in front bowing down so that their fellows in the rear could see the parade.

When the cavalcade reached the vicinity of the palace, it became apparent that the regent still had not given up the effort to hold the reception at some less august place. The palace gates were closed, and the regent made signs that the Americans should go to his house instead. Wells Williams, seeing through their scheme, would not be deterred; he marched straight up to the gate and halted while a messenger scurried around to open it and admit the Americans.

Once inside the palace, Perry and his party were ushered to a hall called "the elevated enclosure of fragrant festivities." Neither the queen, if queen there was, nor the young prince was present; clearly it had been expected that the Americans would fall for the regent's ruse. Refreshments, hastily thrown together, consisted only of stale gingerbread and tea. But the Commodore sat through it grimly. After a decent interval of polite conversation, during which Perry invited the dignitaries to visit him aboard the *Susquehanna*, and offered to supply from his fleet anything they needed, he at last consented to accompany the regent to his home.

There a great feast had indeed been prepared. It consisted of twenty-four courses, double the number usually offered to visiting royalty, but the Americans, though they tried manfully, had to stop at twelve. "On each table," the *Narrative* relates, "were dishes to the number of some twenty, of various sizes and shapes, and the exact basis of some of which no American knoweth to this day; *possibly* it was pig." Evidently the Americans had trouble with chopsticks, for they were provided with small, sharpened bamboo sticks to be used as forks. Some of them crudely mistook these for toothpicks.

But the affair passed off smoothly enough. Perry, offering a toast to the royal family, raised his cup of sake, the chief alcoholic drink of Japan. "Prosperity to the Lew Chewans," he said, "and may they and the Americans always be friends." Next he proposed the health of the regent and his suite, to which the latter replied by toasting the Commodore and his officers. Just before noon, the feast over, the procession formed again and wound its way down to the water. Four of the younger officers, apparently feeling the effects of the sake, brought up the rear with much laughter, riding on bucking native ponies.

On June 28—Perry in the interim having visited and charted the nearby Bonin Islands—the Ryukyuan officials made their return visit aboard the *Susquehanna*. A new regent appeared this time, the old one having resigned because of his advanced age. The successor, a much younger man of about forty-five with a cast in his left eye, seemed uncomfortable and not yet accustomed to his new dignity. His companions, among them his treasurers and the mayor of Naha, were more at their ease, and as the wines and whiskies continued to flow, all reserve melted away. Even the regent, though he never unbent as much as the others did, seemed pleased when Perry, as a parting present, offered him a selection of American garden seeds and vegetables.

The Commodore now felt he had accomplished his purpose in coming to the Ryukyus. He had learned something about the customs and, more important, the attitudes of the people

Although the Japanese had no navy to patrol the islands, reports of approaching foreign ships were brought home by swift, high-sided junks like this one.

and their rulers. He now had reliable charts not only of the Ryukyus but of the Bonins as well. He felt he could with perfect safety leave a ship behind to serve as a kind of floating base until he returned from his first visit to Japan. This assignment fell to the little *Supply*. On the morning of July 2, 1853, the steamers *Mississippi* and *Susquehanna*, towing the sloops *Saratoga* and *Plymouth* (which had arrived in June), upped anchor and departed for the home islands of Japan.

As they sailed northward, word of their coming flew before them. The annual report to the shogun from the Dutch *opperhoofd* at Nagasaki had noted the marshalling of an American squadron at Singapore under "a person named Perry," and had accurately forecast that they would stop at the Ryukyus before proceeding to Japan. At Naha, the Commodore had noticed a flotilla of junks leaving the harbor; he deduced, quite correctly, that they would report his imminent arrival to the Japanese authorities. If he had entertained any hope that surprise would give him an edge, the hope was now gone.

65

4 THE PRESIDENT'S LETTER

Gunners at the ready, leadsmen in the chains sounding the depths, the four American ships—*Susquehanna*, *Mississippi*, *Saratoga*, and *Plymouth*—rounded Cape Sagami on July 8 and at five o'clock in the afternoon let go their anchors off the town of Uraga. Visible to the west was the snow-tipped summit of Japan's sacred mountain, Fuji; just ahead, where the channel widened, lay the great bay leading to Edo itself.

On the flagship Old Matt hoisted a signal: "Have no communication with shore; allow none from shore." Numbers of swift, graceful little Japanese boats clustered about his ships. They had proved a great nuisance to Commodore Biddle, for their curious sailors had swarmed aboard by the score, poking into everything. Perry would have none of that. When the Japanese sought to board, they were fended off with pikes and bayonets. The lines they tried to throw aboard were promptly thrown back again. A

SPENCER COLLECTION, N. Y. PUBLIC LIBRARY

On July 8, 1853, Perry's four black ships halted beneath the bristling shore batteries at Uraga, Japan. A local artist painted the fleet anchored a few hundred yards offshore.

JAPAN EXPEDITION PRESS.

U. S. STEAM-FRIGATE "POWHATAN," SIMODA, JAPAN, MAY 1st, 1854.

LETTER FROM THE PRESIDENT OF THE UNITED STATES.

MILLARD FILLMORE,
PRESIDENT OF THE UNITED STATES OF AMERICA,
To his IMPERIAL MAJESTY,
THE EMPEROR OF JAPAN.
Great and Good Friend!

I send you this public letter by Commodore Matthew C. Perry, an officer of the highest rank in the Navy of the United States, and commander of the squadron now visiting your Imperial Majesty's dominions.

I have directed Commodore Perry to assure your Imperial Majesty that I entertain the kindest feelings towards your Majesty's person and government; and that I have no other object in sending him to Japan, but to propose to your Imperial Majesty that the United States and Japan should live in friendship, and have commercial intercourse with each other.

The constitution and laws of the United States forbid all interference with the religious or political concerns of other nations. I have particularly charged Commodore Perry to abstain from every act which could possibly disturb the tranquillity of your Imperial Majesty's dominions.

The United States of America reach from ocean to ocean, and our territory of Oregon and state of California lie directly opposite to the dominions of your Imperial Majesty. Our steam-ships can go from California to Japan in eighteen days.

Our great state of California produces about sixty millions of dollars in gold, every year, besides silver, quicksilver, precious stones, and many other valuable articles. Japan is also a rich and fertile country, and produces many very valuable articles. Your Imperial Majesty's subjects are skilled in many of the arts. I am desirous that our two countries should trade with each other, for the benefit both of Japan and the United States.

We know that the ancient laws of your Imperial Majesty's government do not allow of foreign trade except with the Dutch. But as the state of the world changes, and new governments are formed, it seems to be wise from time to time to make new laws. There was a time when the ancient laws of your Imperial Majesty's government were first made.

About the same time, America, which is sometimes called the New World, was first discovered and settled by the Europeans. For a long time there were but a few people, and they were poor. They have now become quite numerous; their commerce is very extensive; and they think that if your Imperial Majesty were so far to change the ancient laws as to allow a free trade between the two countries, it would be extremely beneficial to both.

If your Imperial Majesty is not satisfied that it would be safe, altogether, to abrogate the ancient laws which forbid foreign trade, they might be suspended for five or ten years, so as to try the experiment. If it does not prove as beneficial as was hoped, the ancient laws can be restored. The United States often limit their treaties with foreign states to a few years, and then renew them or not, as they please.

I have directed Commodore Perry to mention another thing to your Imperial Majesty. Many of our ships pass every year from California to China; and great numbers of our people pursue the whale fishery near the shores of Japan. It sometimes happens in stormy weather that one of our ships is wrecked on your Imperial Majesty's shores. In all such cases we ask and expect, that our unfortunate people should be treated with kindness, and that their property should be protected, till we can send a vessel and bring them away. We are very much in earnest in this.

Commodore Perry is also directed by me to represent to your Imperial Majesty that we understand there is a great abundance of coal and provisions in the empire of Japan. Our steam-ships, in crossing the great ocean, burn a great deal of coal, and it is not convenient to bring it all the way from America. We wish that our steam-ships and other vessels should be allowed to stop in Japan and supply themselves with coal, provisions and water. They will pay for them, in money, or anything else your Imperial Majesty's subjects may prefer; and we request your Imperial Majesty to appoint a convenient port in the southern part of the empire, where our vessels may stop for this purpose. We are very desirous of this.

These are the only objects for which I have sent Commodore Perry with a powerful squadron to pay a visit to your Imperial Majesty's renowned city of Yedo: friendship, commerce, a supply of coal, and provisions and protection for our shipwrecked people.

We have directed Commodore Perry to beg your Imperial Majesty's acceptance of a few presents. They are of no great value in themselves, but some of them may serve as specimens of the articles manufactured in the United States, and they are intended as tokens of our sincere and respectful friendship.

May the Almighty have your Imperial Majesty in his great and holy keeping!

In witness whereof I have caused the great seal of the United States to be hereunto affixed, and have subscribed the same with my name, at the city of Washington in America, the seat of my government, on the thirteenth day of the month of November, in the year one thousand eight hundred and fifty-two.

Your Good Friend,
MILLARD FILLMORE.
By the President.
EDWARD EVERETT,
Secretary of State.

bold few who started shinnying up the anchor hawsers were shaken off into the waters of the bay.

Finally, however, a boat that had the look of authority came alongside the *Susquehanna*. From its stern flew a black-and-white striped flag; its crew wore what seemed to be official uniforms. And from its deck a voice was heard to say, in clear English, "I can speak Dutch." That, it turned out, was all the English this Japanese interpreter knew, but he did know Dutch. And fortunately, in addition to Wells Williams, Perry had brought along another interpreter, H. A. L. Portman, who was fluent in Dutch.

Portman dutifully relayed the orders he had been given by the Commodore—no one was to be received on board any ship of the squadron save the *Susquehanna*; the American commander was an officer of the highest rank in the Navy "and could confer only with the highest in rank at Uraga." The Japanese replied that the vice-governor was in his boat. Where was the governor himself, Portman wanted to know. The laws of the empire forbade him from going aboard any foreign ship, it was explained. Could not the august foreign lord appoint someone of like rank to confer with the vice-governor?

The Commodore did—Flag Lieutenant Contee—and Nagashima Saberosuke, a Japanese introduced as the vice-governor, climbed up the gangway with his interpreter. They were immediately led below and received in the captain's cabin. Perry remained in his own adjoining cabin, and spoke to the Japanese only through Contee.

The lieutenant explained to them that the Commodore bore a letter from the President of the United

President Fillmore's letter to the emperor was a curious mixture of threats, entreaties, and swaggering bravado. At left is a copy printed aboard the Powhatan, *which joined the squadron in late August. Perry could not be certain if the note would be accepted or if his ships would be attacked. Within plain view were the Japanese shore guns shown in the plan of Uraga harbor at right.*

COLLECTION OF TSUNEO TAMBA, YC-8

69

States to the emperor of Japan, and that he wanted to present it, for transmittal, to an official equal in rank to himself. Nagashima replied that the Japanese could conduct business with foreigners only at Nagasaki; if the Americans would go back there, perhaps the letter could be received and delivered.

Lieutenant Contee was adamant; the Commodore had come to Uraga precisely because it was near the capital, and under no circumstances would he go down to Nagasaki. The letter would have to be received here. Furthermore, the Commodore did not like all those guard boats surrounding his ships. The Japanese were to get rid of them or Perry would order his gunners to open fire.

As soon as this last demand had been translated, Nagashima got up from his seat, walked to the *Susquehanna*'s rail, and ordered the boats to disperse. Most complied, but a few lingered. An armed cutter from the flagship soon scattered them with a show of force. Perry had won his first important concession; never during the remainder of his visit would he be threatened by these bothersome boats.

Nagashima left with his interpreter soon afterward. He was not empowered to make any promises about receiving the President's letter, he said, but next morning "an officer of higher rank" would visit the ship and give an answer.

Perry's sailors and marines spent an

Impressed by Perry's strategy of personal seclusion, the Japanese (one of whom was responsible for this startling portrait) dubbed him "Lord of the Forbidden Interior."

COLLECTION OF DEWOLF PERRY

This "black ship of evil mien," possibly the Susquehanna, *was drawn by one of the many artists dispatched by the Japanese officials to keep a visual record of Perry's activities.*

uneasy night. During the afternoon they had seen rockets fired from the surrounding hills, where Japanese forts—fully manned—were plainly visible. As darkness fell, beacon fires were lighted on the heights, and on shore a bell sounded at regular intervals. Old Matt took no chances. Sentinels were stationed fore and aft and at the gangway of every ship, with ammunition and equipment, ready if necessary to defend the squadron. But there were no incidents that night.

The next morning at seven, as Japanese soldiers marched and countermarched in plain sight of the squadron, two large boats shipped oars at the *Susquehanna*'s gangway. Apparently the law forbidding the governor of Uraga from boarding foreign ships —if there was such a law—had been repealed overnight. For now, Kayama Yezaimon, announced as the governor, presented himself and his entourage. Appointed to receive the dignitaries were Captain Buchanan and Commander Henry Adams.

Unknown to either the Americans or the Japanese, there was comical de-

71

ception on both sides. Perry had represented himself as the highest officer in the U.S. Navy, which of course he was not; but the Japanese thereafter referred to him as "Admiral," and he did nothing to set them right. The Japanese were also playing unaccustomed roles. Kayama was not the governor of Uraga at all; he was merely the prefect of police, upgraded by the shogun especially for the purposes of negotiation, and Nagashima was his assistant. Each side was trying to impress and outbluff the other.

The conference got under way. President Fillmore's letter—written on fine vellum, sealed with gold, and encased in a beautiful rosewood box —was shown to Kayama. It simply could not be received here, he insisted; even if it were, it would have to go through Nagasaki before being sent to the emperor. The squadron really must go down to Nagasaki.

Still secluding himself in his cabin, Perry replied through his deputies that he would not go to Nagasaki. He told them that if they would not appoint someone of suitable rank to receive the President's letter and his own credentials at Uraga, he would deliver them in person. The Japanese stated that they would have to send to Edo for instructions, a round trip of four days. Perry gave them three; they had until Tuesday, July 12, to return with an answer.

As the conference continued, four fully armed surveying boats—one from each American ship—were proceeding up the bay (remaining, however, within range of the ships' guns).

Edward Yorke McCauley, acting master of the Powhatan, *did these sketches during an alert—or "boarding school" as he called it—off the coast of Japan. The four men standing at the ready are from the* Powhatan's *crew. "Sweet Bessie," a giant 64-pounder, was bolted to her foredeck.*

Perry wanted accurate soundings of the bay, of course, but he was also putting subtle pressure on the Japanese by inching closer toward Edo.

On Monday, July 11, taking additional steps to insure that his ultimatum would not be ignored, the Commodore sent the *Mississippi* even farther up the bay. When Kayama came aboard to ask why, he was told that the *Mississippi* was seeking a larger anchorage in case the squadron did not successfully conclude its business and had to return with more ships the following year.

The next day, on schedule, Kayama again appeared, to confer with Buchanan and Adams. A meeting place would be set up on shore, he promised, and an official of high rank appointed to receive the President's letter. It would then be taken to Nagasaki and transmitted through the Dutch or Chinese to the emperor.

Perry, in his inner sanctum, must have been fuming. He sat down and put his answer in writing, giving instructions that it be translated into Dutch and made absolutely clear to the Japanese emissaries: "The Commander-in-chief will not go to Nagasaki, and will receive no communication through the Dutch or Chinese.

"He has a letter from the President of the United States to deliver to the

73

Emperor of Japan, or to his secretary of foreign affairs, and he will deliver the original to none other:—if this friendly letter of the President to the Emperor is not received and duly replied to, he will consider his country insulted, and will not hold himself accountable for the consequences.

"He expects a reply of some sort in a few days, and he will receive such reply nowhere but in this neighborhood [Bay of Uraga]."

The same afternoon, after a quick trip to shore, Kayama was back, this time with two interpreters. The letter would be received on shore near Uraga by a Japanese dignitary bearing proper credentials from the emperor and by him transmitted directly. The day for the reception was designated as Thursday, July 14.

"The squadron was full of bustle," wrote Wells Williams on the appointed morning, "getting arms burnished, boats ready, steam up, men dressed and making all the preparations necessary to go ashore and be prepared for any alternative." For nearly a year the men had anticipated this day. Now it was here. The morale of the expedition—as it prepared to set foot on Japanese soil for the first time—was high.

Very early the two American steamers moved down the bay and anchored off Uraga in broadside formation so that their guns could command the landing area. During the night those on watch had heard the mysterious pounding of hammers on shore, and as the reception place came into view the mystery was cleared up. A special shed had been hastily erected. Evidently it had been prefabricated and transported to Uraga for assembling; several members of the landing party later noticed that the beams still bore markings instructing the carpenters how to fit them together.

An American survey boat, escorted by scores of menacing Japanese craft, makes an exploratory cruise up Edo Bay in 1853. To put pressure on the Japanese, Perry ordered his men to make a show of rowing to Edo itself.

Behind the main shed, there were two smaller ones connected by horizontally-striped curtains of blue and white, held up by stakes driven into the ground. The curtains continued for nearly a mile along the beach in both directions, and horsemen were stationed behind some of them. Altogether, counting cavalry and foot soldiers, there were some 5,000 Japanese troops on hand.

In the center of the little group of buildings, before a crescent of brightly tinted banners, stood nine tall flagpoles, each with a large pennant of deep scarlet reaching down to the ground. The horses, the gay flags, and the little temporary pavilion standing in the open had a medieval air that made the clerk of the *Mississippi* feel like "a spectator of some joust or tourney."

Shortly before ten o'clock, two boats bearing "Governor" Kayama Yezaimon and "Vice-governor" Nagashima Saberosuke arrived alongside the *Susquehanna* to escort the Americans ashore. Both men were dressed in elaborate brocade trimmed with velvet and gold lace. Nagashima, whose broad, short trousers and black woolen socks showed beneath his

COLLECTION OF J. WILLIAM MIDDENDORF II

robe, looked uncomfortable and comic. "He had," according to the *Narrative*, ". . . very much the appearance of an unusually brilliant knave of trumps."

Led by their escort, fifteen American launches and cutters set out from the flagship carrying about a hundred marines, a like number of sailors, forty officers, and forty musicians. Bringing up the rear was the barge of the Commodore, who showed himself to the Japanese now for the first time. Under a salute of thirteen guns from the flagship, he stepped into his barge, stiffly buttoned up to the neck, his sword and epaulets glinting in the sun. The other officers had played upon Perry's vanity to persuade him that he alone should wear a full-dress uniform, so as to appear more splendid than any other American present; actually, they wanted no part of the heavy dress blues in the July heat.

The imposing armada reached shore, and each boat, after landing its men on a pier of sandbags and rice straw, pulled back about fifty feet and dropped its anchor. The crews had orders to keep a sharp lookout and be ready to dash to their comrades' relief in case of trouble on shore. Behind them in the bay the decks of the sloops and frigates were cleared for action. Every man in the landing party had been issued several rounds of ammunition, and their cartridge boxes were full. "Any treachery on [the Japanese] part," Wells Williams wrote, "would have met a serious revenge."

But apparently there was to be no

Perry is portrayed as a bewhiskered swaggerer (above, center) in this view of the Americans parading ashore at Uraga in 1853. Ahead of the Commodore and his oddly undisciplined honor guard march two boys, who appear to be mere toddlers, carrying his credentials and the letter from the President.
BOEHRINGER COLLECTION; MARINERS MUSEUM

OVERLEAF: *Blaring "Hail Columbia," Perry's band (center) marches resolutely at the head of the procession bearing President Fillmore's note; waiting for it is the governor of Uraga, seated beside a cannon in the enclosure. This painting, however crude, does capture the splendor of the event.*
COLLECTION OF CARL H. BOEHRINGER

長二間
横六間
下曹

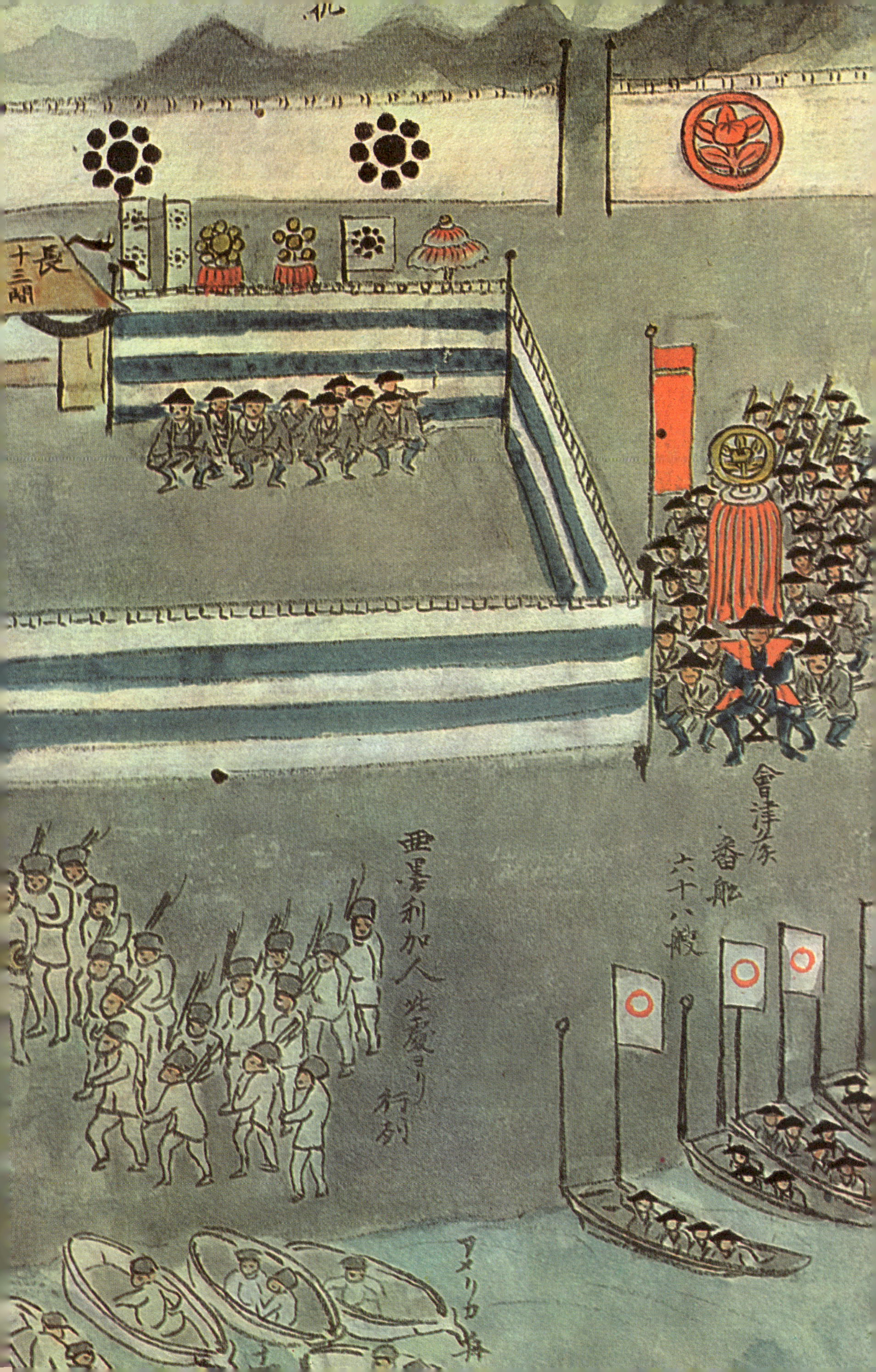

長
十三間
會津侯
番船
六十八艘
亜墨利加人此處ヨリ
行列
アメリカ船

The reception, drawn by Heine, was the culmination of months of preparation. It lasted about thirty minutes, most of which were spent in awkward silence.

treachery. The marines, all spit and polish, were at the head of the procession. Then came a powerfully-built sailor carrying Perry's colors, followed by two boys bearing the President's letter. Behind them waited the resplendent Commodore, flanked by two stalwart jack-tars with American flags attached to tall pikes. Next in line were the officers of the fleet, comfortable in their undress uniforms, and last were the hundred sailors and forty bandsmen, wearing blue caps with red, white, and blue bands. The musicians struck up "Hail, Columbia," an officer barked a command, and the grand procession stepped off smartly toward the meetinghouse.

Once inside the chamber—carpeted in red and hung with violet-colored draperies—the Commodore and his aides were ushered to stiff-backed chairs. Kayama and Nagashima introduced the two officials appointed to receive the American documents: Toda, "Prince of Idzu," an intellectual-looking man of about fifty; and Ido, "Prince of Iwami," a wizened individual of about sixty-five. They sat in state opposite the Americans, and scarcely spoke throughout the ceremony.

The letter and credentials were brought forward, displayed to the

Japanese, and deposited in a red lacquered box standing on gilt legs in the center of the room. Through Kayama, Ido transmitted the official receipt and reply, which read as follows: "The letter of the President of the United States of North America, and copy, are hereby received, and will be delivered to the Emperor.

"It has been many times intimated that business relating to foreign countries cannot be transacted here in Uraga, but at Nagasaki; nevertheless, as it has been observed that the Admiral, in his quality as ambassador of the President, would feel himself insulted by a refusal to receive the letter at this place, the justice of which has been acknowledged, the above mentioned letter is hereby received, in opposition to the Japanese laws.

"As this is not a place wherein to negotiate with foreigners, so neither can conferences nor entertainment be held. Therefore, as the letter has been received, you can depart."

An awkward silence ensued. Finally, Perry said that he was about to sail for the Ryukyus and the China coast; he would gladly carry any messages his hosts wished delivered. There being no reply, he added that he intended to return to Japan the following year, possibly in April or May. Would he bring all his ships with him? "All of them," he replied, "and probably more, as these are only a portion of the squadron." Kayama and Nagashima stepped forward, closed the red box, and informed Perry's interpreters that the interview was over.

As the Commodore and his suite stood up to leave, Ido and Toda bowed deeply, their faces impassive. Wells Williams, describing the incident in his diary, wrote: "I got the impression that the two high men had pursed themselves up to an attitude, and had taken on this demure look as part of it. . . ." He was right; the two "princes" had been acting. They were not princes at all, but merely provincial governors—temporarily promoted, like the police chief and his assistant, to deal with the foreigners.

That last phrase of the Japanese receipt—"as the letter has been received, you can depart"—had not sat well with the starchy Commodore, and he was determined to show these people how little he thought of their ultimatum. When his officers and men were safely aboard the ships, he gave orders that the squadron was to move up into Edo Bay itself, surveying boats out ahead.

Kayama Yezaimon came aboard, agitated, to ask why the "Admiral" was doing this; he had promised that after his papers had been received he would leave. Through his subordinates Perry reminded the interpreter that he had promised only to leave the *shore*; he had said nothing about leaving the country. Besides, he reminded Kayama, he had told him that he planned to return next year, and that a larger fleet would require a

Based on maps and information secretly furnished by a Japanese official, this rough chart of Edo Bay is from the log of Edward McCauley. The numbers indicate various depths by fathoms.

better anchorage than had been found off Uraga. Perry did find a suitable mooring in Edo Bay, and dubbed it "American Anchorage." Not until Sunday morning, July 17, did the four American ships sail away.

It had been a most profitable eight days. Writing in his diary on the evening following the reception, Wells Williams summed it up very well: ". . . thus closed this eventful day, one which will be a day to be noted in the history of Japan, one on which the key was put into the lock and a beginning made to do away with the long seclusion of this nation, for I incline to think that the reception of such a letter in such a public manner involves its consideration if not its acceptance...."

Stopping at the Ryukyu Islands on his way back to China, the Commodore had an opportunity to make sure that that way station would remain open to American interests. He instructed Commander Adams and Wells Williams to inform the regent and his council bluntly that they would be wise "to abrogate those laws and customs which are not suited to the present age, and which they have no power to enforce."

Despite this bluster, the regent's written reply, delivered at a meeting on July 28, 1853, was evasive. Perry ordered the letter handed back as unsatisfactory. The regent had until noon the next day to come to his senses, Perry said; otherwise a force of two hundred men would land, march to the palace, and hold it until satisfaction was forthcoming.

The Commodore was bluffing—he admitted later that he had no intention of using force—but the bluff was never called. As one observer put it, the islanders knew that they were "in the talons of the eagle." All of the American terms were accepted, and Perry had won a secure base on the threshold of Japan.

The Commodore now began to plan for the next year's return to the Japanese capital. He left the Ryukyus for the China coast, where he would refit and gather the rest of his fleet. Perry reached the mainland to learn that the international fracas which had earlier engaged the *Susquehanna* and delayed his first departure for Japan was still going on. Certain Chinese leaders were determined to sweep all foreign interests from the coasts of their country. Chinese freebooters attacked the foreign *hongs*, or commercial houses, and the harbors and rivers were infested with pirates who, in the words of Perry's biographer, "could steal the copper bottom off a full-rigged ship." For the next five months much of Perry's force was engaged in protecting American traders from these

OVERLEAF: *To obtain a "perfect, permanent, and universal Peace," Perry returned to Japan in early 1854, dropping anchor off Kanagawa on February 25. There, one of the ever-present Japanese artists painted this scene.*

COLLECTION OF MR. AND MRS. HAROLD S. GREHAN, JR.

本牧本郷村
之内八王子山
より十二天之見
因州様
御固

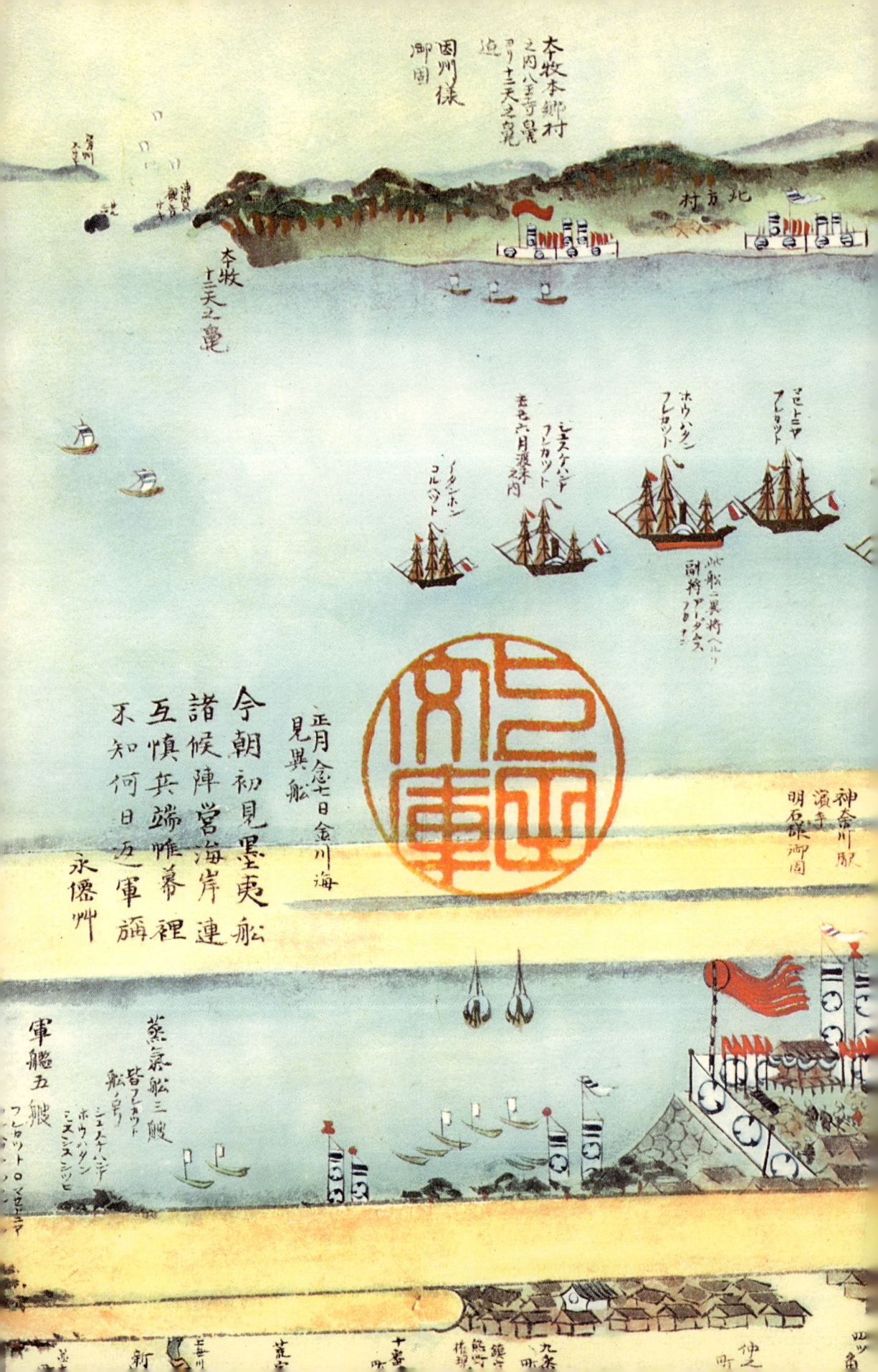

北本牧村

本牧十二天之亀

マヒトヤフレガット
ホウハタンフレガット
去ル六月渡来之内
シエスケハンフレカット
ノタホンコルヘット
此船ニ異将ヘルリ
副将アダムス乗ル

神奈川駅
演手
明石様御固

正月念七日金川海
見異船

今朝初見墨夷船
諸候陣営海岸連
互慎兵端唯幕裡
不知何日近軍艦
永儜州

軍艦五艘
フレガットロマセユミヤ
蒸気船三艘
皆フレガット
シエスケハンテ
ホウハツン
シスンスシツプ

横濱村
御固
小笠原様
真田様

横濱
水神社
異人旅籠御場所
横濱新田
開洲弁天
ハシマ
入江
戸部堤

二月十八日異人
台場二十六人
ハッテイラ十二艘
三ヶ所ゟ上陸

ハンクリヤ
コルヘット

サラトガ
コルヘット
去ル六月渡来之内

レキシントン
コルヘット

権現山

神奈川ゟ横濱応接
之御場所迄海上九里

漁師町

青木台町

小傳馬町

御本陣

瀧之町

栗町

These sketches of the Kanagawa anchorage show the position of Perry's ships on the morning of the "Great Landing." John Lewis, who with his twin brother joined the Navy to see Japan, fashioned the "off hand scrawl" above.

attacks. Toward the end of 1853, before the Chinese pirates had been wholly routed, he assembled his squadron at Hong Kong for the voyage to Japan.

Old Matt had not intended to go until sometime in April or May, but now events were forcing him to hurry. At the end of November a French frigate at Macao suddenly put to sea under sealed orders. About the same time, a Russian admiral named Pontiatine, with a fleet of four vessels, arrived at Shanghai from Nagasaki. Perry strongly suspected that both the French and Russians intended to go to Japan and take advantage of the wedge he himself had driven. He determined to risk the bad weather prevalent in those waters in winter, and leave as soon as he could. Anxiously, he awaited the arrival of the storeship *Lexington*, which was bringing the presents he intended for the Japanese. She finally reached Hong Kong on December 26.

On the day set for Perry's departure, an unwelcome letter arrived from the Secretary of the Navy. A new American commissioner, R. M. McLane, was on the way to China, and Perry was ordered to assign one of his steamers to support McLane's mission. Here was a fine dilemma. The Commodore was ready to leave for Japan; he had, in fact, already dispatched some of his slower vessels for the Ryukyus, where the full squadron was to rendezvous. To lose at this point one of his precious steamers—which had impressed the Japanese far more than the sailing ships—was unthinkable.

Old Matt sat down and wrote a bold answer to the Secretary's letter. He would send back a steamer after he got to Edo, he said, but he could not spare one now. "I must confess," he added, "that this order has damped my hopes very much...." So saying, he proceeded to ignore it, and on January 14 he set sail for Japan.

The fleet, which assembled off Kanagawa on February 25, included the steamers *Mississippi*, *Susquehanna*, and *Powhatan*; the sloops *Vandalia* and *Macedonian*; and the storeships *Lexington* and *Southampton*. With the arrival of the *Saratoga* and the *Supply* in March, Perry would have more than 120 guns and 1,800 men. If force should be required to open the door he had pushed ajar, he thought he would have enough.

87

5

Mustering all available men, and parading them with the skill of a showman, Perry landed proudly and noisily at Kanagawa, providing a spectacle the Japanese thronged to see.

"ALL THE SAME HEART"

March 8, 1854, the day appointed for the opening of negotiations, dawned fine and clear. Half an hour before noon, twenty-seven boats loaded with nearly five hundred armed Americans—officers and sailors, the bands of the three steamers, and all the marines that could be spared—put off from the ships and rowed for shore. Under an ambassador's salute of seventeen guns, Commodore Perry stepped into his white barge and followed his men to the beach.

The awestruck cabin boy of the sloop *Vandalia* described the colorful landing: ". . . It was an imposing sight to see the bluff, burly Commodore marching up between the bristling ranks, bareheaded and surrounded by his staff . . . sailors and soldiers presenting arms—the officers saluting—the bands from the various ships playing national airs . . . and last tho' not least the strange dresses, arms, and looks of the natives who came from all parts of the empire to view [this] strange, and to them, wonderful sight." The expedition's official artist, Wilhelm Heine, was ordered to sketch the scene, and to put

COLLECTION OF J. WILLIAM MIDDENDORF II

the Commodore in the middle of it.

Twenty-four days earlier, on February 13, the Americans had returned from the China coast to Japan, as Perry had promised; their mission was to demand an answer to the President's letter and to negotiate a treaty. The Commodore had no way of knowing that during his six-month absence Japan had undergone startling changes which would make his task immeasurably easier.

The first hint of change had come when the squadron sailed up Edo Bay. No guard boats had appeared to harass the black ships, nor had any rockets been fired from the forts along the shore. Without hindrance the fleet had moved directly up to the "American Anchorage," ten miles above Uraga.

Another sign of change was that, in the three weeks between the Americans' arrival and their landing, the Japanese had been unfailingly friendly. On March 1, Captain Buchanan gave a dinner aboard the *Susquehanna* for Kayama Yezaimon, the diplomat who had ably represented the shogun in 1853. Yezaimon and his associates ate—and drank—heartily.

Among the guests was another Japanese diplomat the Americans remembered from the previous year—Nagashima Saberosuke, the comical "knave of trumps." Most of the guests remained sedately seated as the evening drew on, but Nagashima pranced up and down the room, trying on Captain Buchanan's hat and admiring himself in a mirror. At last, he ended his antics by pouring out a glass of salad oil and drinking it down, evidently mistaking it for wine.

The third important evidence of change was that the shipboard negotiations had gone more smoothly than before. It was agreed that the site for the treaty-signing was to be Kana-

Cannon of the ship above and of the launches at right spew forth clouds of smoke in these Japanese drawings. The gunners of Perry's fleet were often ordered to fire such salutes to herald his actions and pronouncements—and to remind the Japanese of the destructive power at his command.

BOTH: LIBRARY OF CONGRESS

gawa, a port which lay opposite the Anchorage, and that a suitable reception hall would be constructed.

Behind this new cordiality on the part of the Japanese diplomats lay a serious crisis within the empire. Even before Perry's first appearance, the Japanese who had favored opening the door to the outside world had grown almost as influential in the capital as the reactionaries who clung to the old ways. The liberals wanted to overthrow the shogun and restore the powers of the emperor.

After Perry had left in 1853, the insecure shogun and his councilors, headed by Lord Abe, took an unusual step. For the first time in almost four centuries they called upon all the nobles of the realm, including those of the emperor's retinue, to seek their advice. What should the government do when Perry came again: fight or negotiate?

Most of the nobles were determined to fight, but their time had passed. Japan had slumbered too long. A hastily conceived rearmament program ended in utter failure. After inspecting an example of Japanese de-

彼理上陸所

fenses, one of the American officers later commented, "The fort, if it can be so called, was nothing but a painted screen intended to hide the warriors from the view of the enemy, behind it were four rows of soldiers . . . apparently as immovable as stone." They were armed with spears, pikes, and ancient matchlock muskets.

To make matters worse, the shogun had died several months before Perry's return. The Tokugawa successor realized his own weakness and knew that he had no choice but to negotiate with the Americans. He appointed a

Perry took pains to insure that his troops looked their spit-and-polish best on shore. The Japanese were quick to see that their own forces were not so well armed or prepared as the Americans. These Japanese drawings show an American officer, drilling a detachment of marines, and Commodore Perry, clutching his hat and dress sword, followed by his large-sized standard-bearer.

93

American participants in and about the negotiations were strange, somewhat comical beings to the Japanese artists who portrayed them. The large figures are (from left) Perry, an interpreter, and a rifleman. The four men caricatured at right are (from top) interpreter H. A. L. Portman, interpreter Wells Williams, Commander Henry Adams, and Lt. Oliver Hazard Perry.

ALL: BOEHRINGER COLLECTION; MARINERS MUSEUM

ALL: NORFOLK MUSEUM

Perry's opposites at the conference were upgraded government officials. These "princes" tried to impress the Americans by means of a resplendent imperial barge (drawn above by an American officer), in which they crossed the bay to Kanagawa.

cabinet that would support him, promoted Kayama Yezaimon for the way he had handled affairs in 1853, and designated as his chief representative at Kanagawa a liberal scholar named Hayashi. Now, on the eighth day of March, Hayashi and his fellow commissioners prepared to embark on a fateful, unalterable course which would open Japan to the world.

Having come ashore with great ceremony at Kanagawa, Perry and his staff marched to the treaty house, a long, low building of unpainted pine. Ascending a flight of three steps, the American delegation went inside. The floor was carpeted with three-inch-thick straw mats, very springy underfoot. The far wall was almost completely covered by a large blue flag with the Tokugawa coat of arms. Along the side walls, hung with paintings, were low benches and tables draped with red cotton cloth. The air still had the nip of early spring, and copper bowls of glowing charcoal heated the room.

The Commodore, his aides, and interpreters Williams and Portman were seated on the left, and soon afterward the five Japanese commissioners entered and bowed. Their chief, Hayashi, introduced to Perry as "Lord Rector" and "prince councilor," was plainly dressed in a dark silk robe. A handsome man of about fifty-five with a grave though pleasant face, he had courtly manners; he took the lead in the conversation with the Americans, and his fellow commissioners plainly deferred to him. Ido, the next in rank, was presented as "Prince of Tsus-shima," though he was only a city magistrate; to Wells Williams he seemed "a gross, sleepy looking man, as much unlike a prince as if he was a chimney-sweeper." Next came Isawa, "Prince of Mema-saki," actually one of the governors of Uraga. At forty he was the youngest of the group; the Commodore thought him the best-looking. As the negotiations wore on, the Americans were to find Isawa a broad-minded, fun-loving individual. When the bands played he could not resist tapping out the tempo with his foot, and he had a reputation as a ladies' man. Udono, a member of the Board of Revenue; Matsusaki, a scholar of Chinese; and two kneeling interpreters rounded out the Japanese treaty team. The most powerful Jap-

COLLECTION OF CARL H. BOEHRINGER

anese present was never introduced to the Americans; Lord Abe himself had come down from Edo to keep an eye on things, and had concealed himself among the lesser officials.

Hayashi opened the proceedings. With great cordiality, he welcomed Perry and congratulated him on having completed a second voyage from distant lands.

The Commodore, equally polite, returned Hayashi's greeting and complimented the "prince councilor" on his good health. In honor of the occasion, Perry announced, "I shall fire a salute of 21 guns in honor of the Princes and 18 guns in honor of the Lord Rector. Another salute of 18 guns will be fired to celebrate my first landing." Out in the bay the guns were duly fired aboard the *Powhatan*, now Perry's flagship, and the Jap-

The value Americans put on all human life, a point emphasized by Perry, became more credible to the Japanese when a marine private was buried with full military honors. Above is a Japanese view of the funeral procession.

anese colors were raised at her peak.

Hayashi: "Last summer, the President sent . . . a letter, which you presented. Among the various requests made in this letter, there were some referring to fuel, water, and provisions. An order has already been issued regarding this matter. As you appear earnestly to desire coal, we will make an exception and supply you with what we have. Further, with regard to the kindly treatment of shipwrecked persons, we have had laws in the past . . . but such persons will be treated with kindness hereafter. We will assent, therefore, to two of these proposals, but the others, regarding trade and so on, we cannot accept."

Perry: ". . . We have in our country always regarded human life as of the first importance . . . and, therefore, whenever any of our countrymen—of course—or persons belonging to another country . . . reach our shores after having been shipwrecked, we exert every effort to rescue them, and we treat them with kindness. I perceive no sign, however, that human life is counted in your country to be of great importance; for whenever a vessel of any foreign country approaches your shores, you repel it with guns; and when shipwrecked persons reach the shore, you treat them like slaves and keep them in harsh imprisonment."

If this sort of treatment continued, Old Matt warned, the United States might come to look upon Japan as an enemy; in that case, war might result. He pointed out that America had just concluded a war—costing dearly in men and arms—with a neighboring country, Mexico. "Circumstances may lead your country into a similar plight," Perry continued. "It would be well for you to reconsider."

Japan was not inhumane, Hayashi countered. It had—and this was a dig at Perry's mention of the Mexican War—been at peace for three hundred years. The "Admiral" must have heard false reports about Japanese treatment of castaways. They were received kindly, taken to Nagasaki, and returned to their own countries with the help of the Dutch. True, some had been "detained temporarily," but only because they had refused to obey Japanese laws. He concluded: "If you in your country truly value human life, you will not allow the resentment of successive years to crystallize. These are not matters so grave as to make war necessary. It would be well for you indeed to reconsider."

Perry was shrewd enough not to pursue this line of argument any further; the Japanese negotiator was too subtle for him. Besides, Hayashi had already agreed to President Fillmore's request that American ships calling at Japanese ports be provisioned and that steamers be coaled. If Hayashi would issue a formal order to that effect, Perry said, he would be satisfied. Now the Commodore tried a new tack. "Why do you not allow commerce?" he asked. "Commerce has to do with the things which a nation has

The shed in which the negotiations were held is shown in this pencil sketch made by midshipman John Glendy Sproston. His crude rendition of the landing ceremony shows Perry, preceded by a pennant carrier and followed by two of his aides, approaching the shed between straight lines of marines and sailors. The group in the background at right is part of a bodyguard for one of the Japanese negotiators.

and with what it lacks; it is a source of great profit... It brings wealth to each country."

"We are not discontented at being without the products of other countries," Hayashi calmly replied. "Having decided that we shall not permit commerce, we cannot easily decide to permit it. You say that your principal purpose in coming was to have greater value placed upon human life and to have help given to ships. You have attained your purposes... Is it not enough that you have gained what you sought?"

Perry paused a moment before answering, choosing his words carefully. "You are right," he replied at last. "As you say, I came because I valued human life, and the important thing is that you will give our vessels help. Commerce brings profit to a country, but it does not concern human life. I shall not insist upon it." The Commodore paused again. Reaching into his pocket, he pulled out a little book, as if to give it to the Japanese. But then, seeming to think better of the idea, he put the book back again. He repeated this trick two or three times, until

The decorum of the American conferees sketched at left by midshipman Sproston contrasts sharply with the distaste and awkwardness of the Navy officers trying to eat raw fish at a dinner, as depicted above by a Japanese. Whether the Commodore and his aides were represented as gentlemen or as barbarians usually depended on the artist's nationality.

OVERLEAF: *The American presents were delivered on March 13 and put on display in a structure adjoining the treaty house. As this drawing indicates, the gifts were chosen more for utility than beauty. The wire-strung poles in the background, looking incongruously modern, were set up by American engineers for their telegraphic demonstrations.*

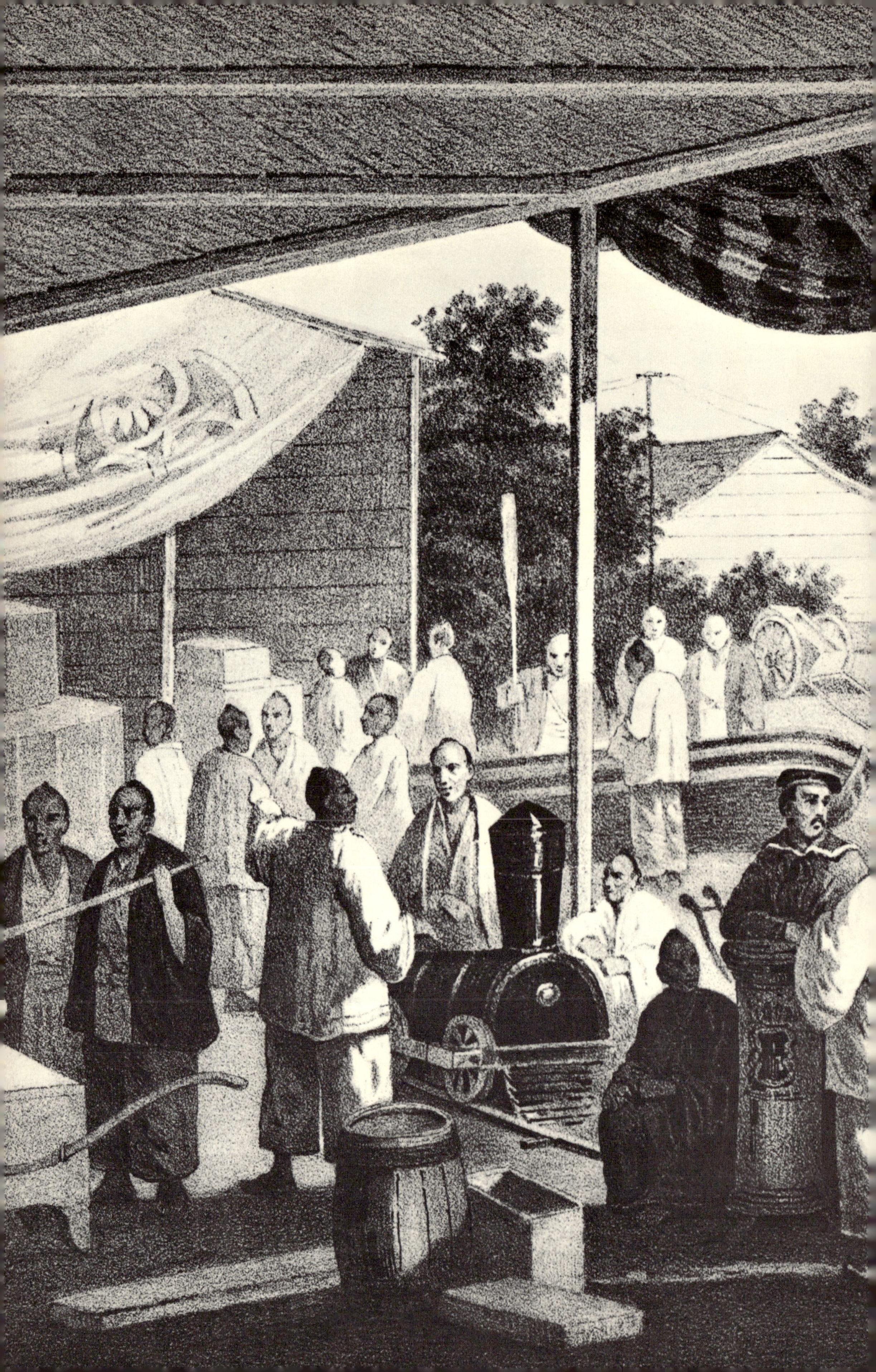

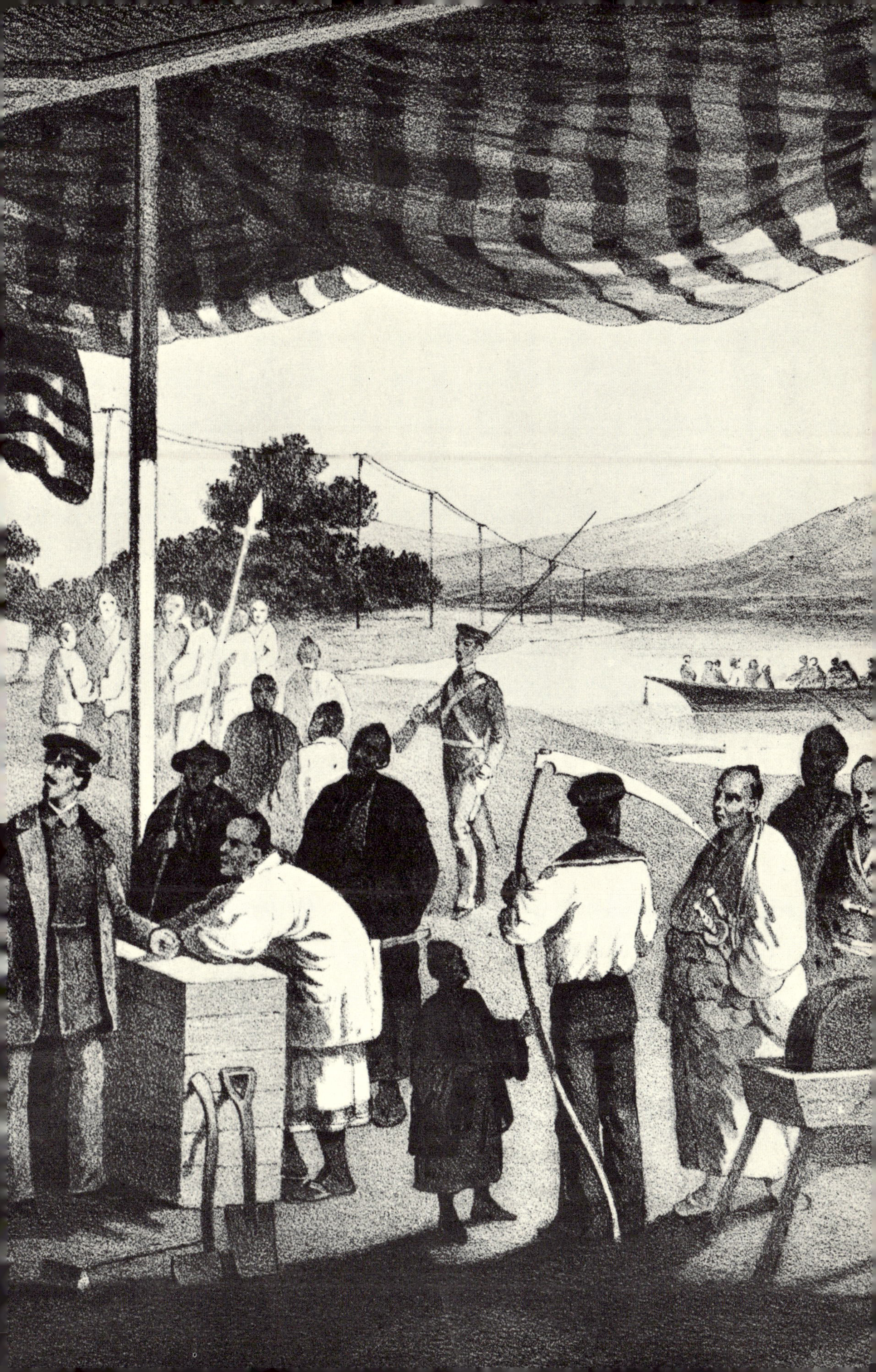

he was certain he had aroused the curiosity of all the Japanese commissioners. Then he explained, almost apologetically, "This book is the treaty made between the United States and China when commerce was first established. I brought it because, if commerce were to be permitted, it would govern this matter fairly . . . but in view of your arguments, I shall not insist. Having brought it, I hope that you will peruse it for your information only." With this he handed over the book, which was printed in Chinese.

Hayashi decided to go along with the game. He replied gravely: "We cannot easily agree to engage in commerce, as I said; but if you desire me merely to peruse your treaty with China, I have no objection to doing so." He took the book, bowed, and gave a sign that the interview was over. Refreshments were served and the other four Japanese sat down with the Americans. Hayashi, however, wishing to show that he outranked Perry, left the hall.

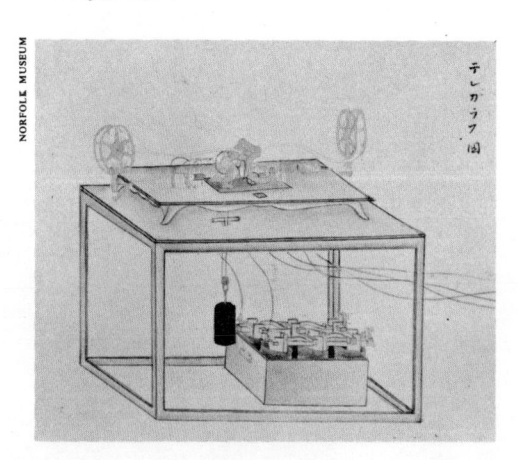

The Japanese concessions as Hayashi had explained them seemed quite generous. But when Perry got back to his ship and the scroll containing the formal answer to the President's letter was translated, he realized that they were not giving up much at all. As Hayashi had promised, American ships would be supplied, but only at one port—which Perry was to select—and that would not be open for five years. Meanwhile, coal would be available at Nagasaki. After asking exactly what the Americans meant by "provisions" and how much coal they would need, the message ended: "After settling the points before mentioned, the treaty can be concluded and signed at the next interview." In other words, the Japanese were doing as little as possible to meet Perry's demands, and they wanted to get rid of him as quickly as they could.

Perry's answer was to demand more, not less, than the President's letter requested. In a message sent ashore with Adams, he asked not for one port, but for five—three of which

None of the Americans' gifts fascinated the Japanese more than the telegraph and the miniature railroad, parts of which are shown here in Japanese prints. Awed officials examined the telegraph wires to see if they were hollow. Nobles, like children at a fair, sat astride the passenger car's roof and sped delightedly around a short circle of track.

were to be opened immediately. If the Japanese did not comply, he threatened them with a "larger force and more stringent terms and instructions." Wells Williams thought the Commodore was pushing too hard; after all, he had already obtained all that Washington had hoped for. In his diary he wrote angrily: "Perry cares no more for right, for consistency, for his country, than will advance his own . . . fame, and makes his ambition the test of all his conduct toward the Japanese." Williams admitted that if the Japanese yielded and did away with the closed-door policy once and for all, great good might come of it. "Yet I despise such papers as this drawn up today," he added, "and it may defeat its own object; it certainly has lowered the opinion I had of its author."

If Perry was aware of his interpreter's disapproval, he showed no sign of it. While the Japanese were thinking over his latest proposal, he decided to bring out the presents he had assembled before leaving the United States. If arguments and threats would not induce the Japanese to agree to trade, perhaps the shiny American gadgets would. The commissioners agreed to come to the treaty house on Monday, March 13, for the presentation ceremony.

Several large boats were required to take the gifts ashore. There was a good cross section of American products—copies of John James Audubon's beautiful drawings of American birds, Noah Webster's dictionaries (for the Japanese interpreters), and maps of North America and of the individual states. There were garden seeds and farm tools, Irish potatoes, champagnes and whiskies, even perfumes "for the Empress." Samuel Colt's pistols were especially popular among the dignitaries.

But the star attractions were the telegraph and the tiny steam railroad. Transmitters and receivers were set up a mile apart, a wire was strung between them, and messages were sent back and forth. Some of the Japanese tried to outrun the messages, but

LIBRARY OF CONGRESS

107

108

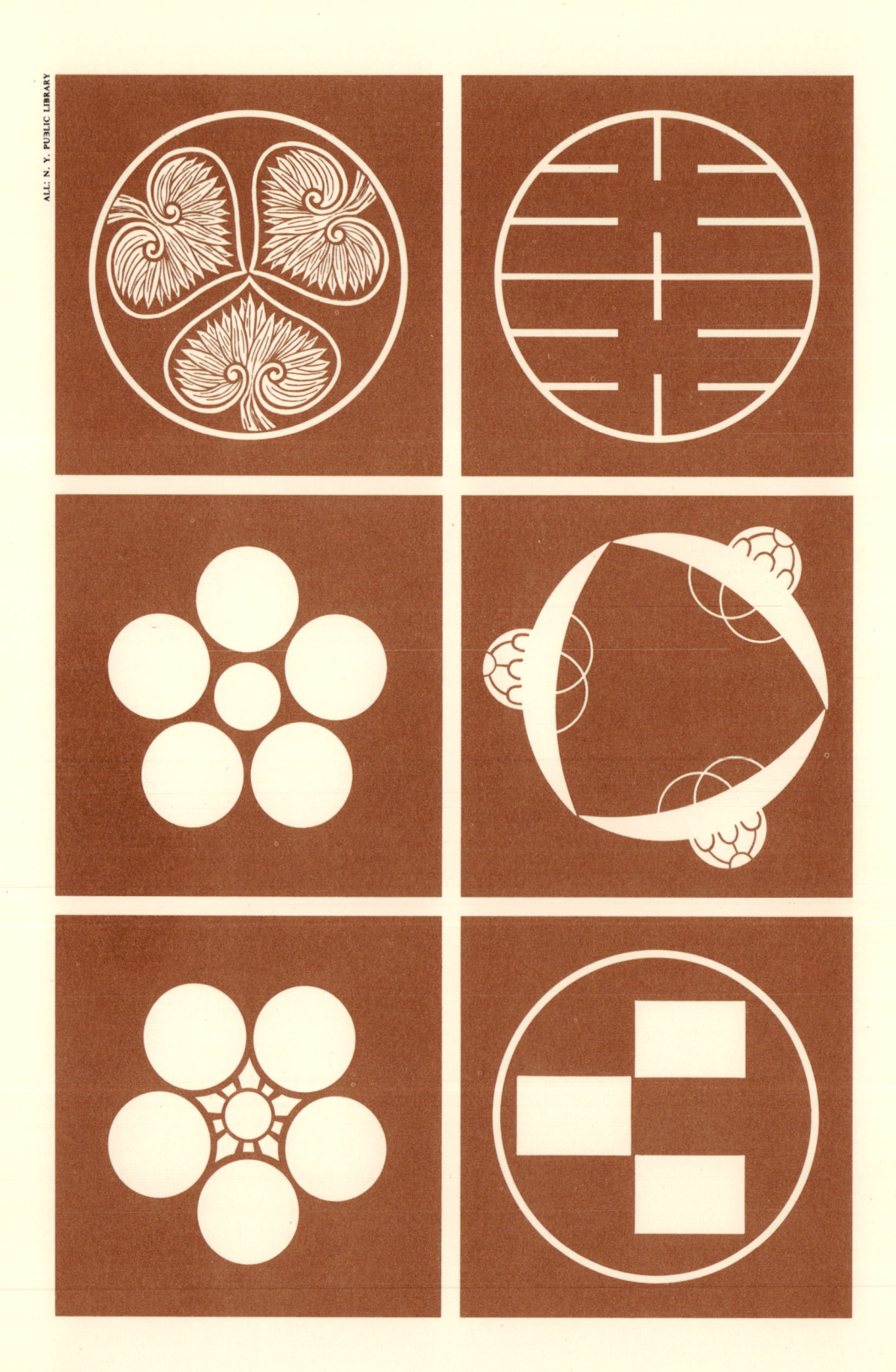

HISTORIOGRAPHICAL INSTITUTE

The emblems of the major Japanese personalities concerned with the negotiations are arranged at left. From left to right and top to bottom, they are those of the emperor, Chief Commissioner Hayashi, and commissioners Ido, Isawa, Tsudsuki, and Udono. Above is Hayashi, described as having "a grave and saturnine expression of face" together with "extremely courtly manners."

when they pulled up huffing and puffing at the other end of the wire, the words were always there before them.

The railroad track was laid in a circle in an open field, and two of the ships' engineers put the locomotive in working order. The little car was too small for even the diminutive Japanese to squeeze inside, but they were not to be cheated out of a ride: they perched on the roof. "It was a spectacle not a little ludicrous," the *Narrative* says, "to behold a dignified mandarin whirling around the circular road at the rate of twenty miles an hour, with his loose robes flying in the wind. As he clung with desperate hold to the edge of the roof, grinning with intense interest, and his huddled-up body shook convulsively with a kind of laughing timidity, the car spun rapidly around the circle."

The curiosity of the lower-ranking Japanese was not limited to the gadgets; they were endlessly fascinated by the Americans' clothes. They followed the officers and men about, inspecting their swords and pistols, fingering the material of their uniforms, even poking curious hands into their pockets. Buttons and buttonholes were entirely new to them; they fastened their own clothing with ties and sashes. A sailor or marine could make himself a hero just by handing out a few buttons, which the Japanese carefully pocketed and took home. And, everywhere, the Americans noticed Japanese with little brushes and sheets of paper, drawing pictures of all that they saw.

109

COLLECTION OF CARL H. BOEHRINGER

The Americans considered the Japanese stingy in their gifts, but a Japanese artist depicted the presentation of silk to three American officers as a fine state occasion.

COLLECTION OF DEWOLF PERRY

A sumo wrestler easily carries two heavy sacks of rice while an American struggles to lift one in the comical Japanese sketch above. The sacks of rice were given to the Americans as traditional imperial gifts; so were the two spotted dogs and the dried fish wrapped in paper, at right. The Japanese matchlock and powder holder, antique but not particularly valuable objects, were given to Perry by the commissioners as special tokens of respect for the U.S. representative.

Back in February, when some of the natives had come aboard the *Susquehanna* to watch the firing of a salute in honor of Washington's birthday, one of them had shown Wells Williams a book containing marvelously accurate drawings of American guns, cannon, and uniforms. It had been published at Edo the previous October, only three months after Perry's first visit. "The Japanese are, undoubtedly . . . a very imitative, adaptive, and compliant people," the *Narrative* notes. "In these characteristics may be discovered a promise of the comparatively easy introduction of foreign customs and habits."

On clear days negotiations continued ashore. Perry and his aides, sensing that there was no longer any danger, dispensed with their armed escort and were more at ease with their hosts. Hayashi still wanted to confine all future dealings with Americans to Nagasaki. Perry firmly opposed the idea; at Nagasaki, he felt, his countrymen would be forced to obey the laws imposed upon the Dutch, and he wanted no part of that legal, but servile, existence. The Commodore, however, did not voice this reason for opposing Nagasaki; he simply said that it was inconvenient. "If you will designate five or six ports in the southeast of Japan," he told Hayashi, "our ships will not fail to put in at these places only, and they will not enter other harbors, which would be to your advantage."

Hayashi: "We cannot set aside a number of places, as you wish; but if Nagasaki is so inconvenient a place, we can select some other suitable harbor in its stead."

Perry: "It would be very inconvenient to have only one harbor. Please set aside three or four at least, one of them to be Kanagawa."

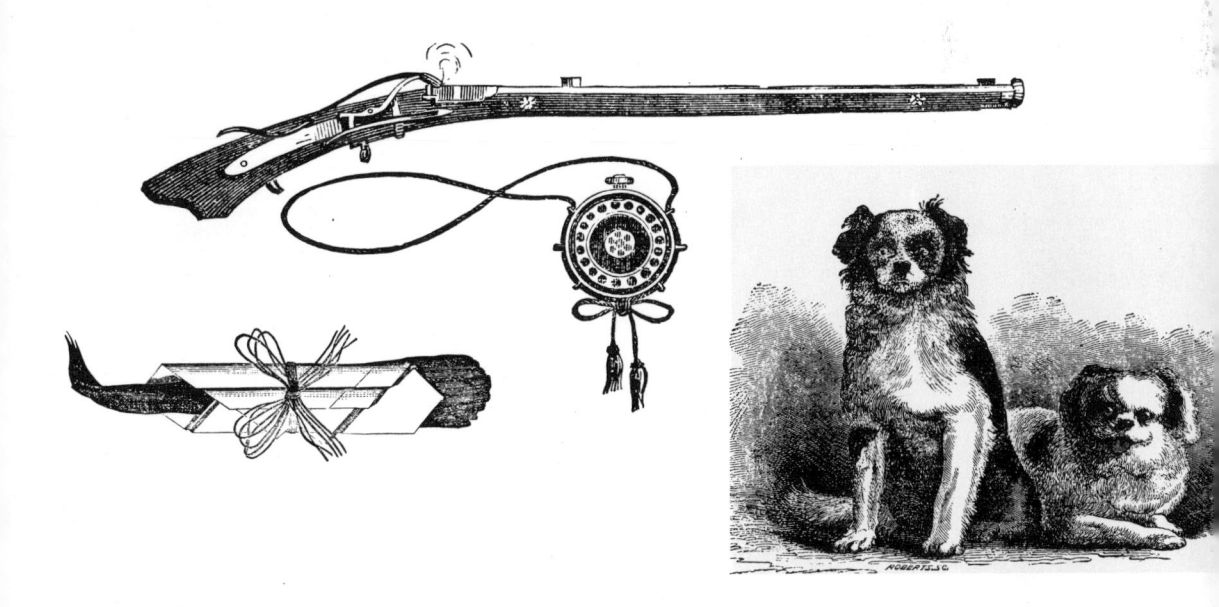

"The Americans were very much surprised," says the writing in the woodblock print below. Actually, the Americans, watching a sumo match, seem as much amused as amazed. At right is one of the huge, much-honored wrestlers, drawn by Edward McCauley. Another of Perry's men described the exhibition fighters as "overfed monsters, whose animal natures had been so carefully developed... that it was easy... to lose all sense of their being human creatures."

Hayashi: "We cannot set aside Kanagawa, but we will surely select a suitable port in the southeast."

Perry: "What harbor will that be?"

Hayashi: "As this is a new proposal, I cannot reply without a thorough investigation."

He was, of course, stalling for time. Any matter as important as treaty ports had to be checked with the government at Edo. Perry seems to have suspected as much, for he said: "I have the power as plenipotentiary to decide these matters in my own discretion, and I cannot believe that you, who are also here as a plenipotentiary, are unable to give an immediate reply to such a question. Please give me an answer at once."

But Hayashi was not to be hurried, and time passed. On March 24 the Japanese commissioners, having gone to Edo themselves to see the shogun, were back with an anwer. Two days later they reported to Perry that the ports of Shimoda, on the island of Honshu in the south, and Hakodate, on Hokkaido in the north, were to be opened. The Commodore had heard of Hakodate, but not of Shimoda; would the Japanese mind if he inspected it before agreeing? "That most surely is a reasonable request," Hayashi replied. The *Vandalia* and the *Southampton* were promptly dispatched.

Since the negotiations were going so well, the Japanese decided to present their gifts to the Americans. Spread out upon the benches and tables in the treaty house was a very pretty array of the lacquerware for which Japanese artisans were justly famous: boxes, tables, trays, writing boxes. There were porcelain cups and vases exquisitely made and beautifully hand-painted. Bolts of flowered silk and cotton, fans, pipe cases, and various articles made of bamboo enhanced the display.

The Americans admitted to one another that the Japanese presents were much more attractively packaged than their own, which had come in wooden crates and plain wrapping paper, but in the gifts themselves they were disappointed. "Not worth over a thousand dollars . . ." wrote Lieutenant George Preble in his diary. "I am sure one of our presents, Audubon's Great work on Am[erican] Birds, was worth more than all we saw there, and that our miniature railroad engine and cars cost several times their value. Everyone, the Commodore included, remarked on the meager display and the lack of rich brocades and magnificent things always associated with our ideas of Japan."

But the Japanese had another surprise for their guests. Taking them out behind the treaty house, the commissioners explained that it was a Japanese custom, when presenting gifts, to give some food as well. Three hundred chickens and two hundred large sacks of rice, each weighing over 125 pounds, had been brought for the galleys of the squadron. To carry these sacks down to the beach, twenty-five huge Japanese now appeared, naked save for loincloths. They picked up the bags with ease, some of them carrying two at a time, and put them in a pile near the American boats. One of the men took a sack of rice in his arms and turned somersaults with it.

These men were sumo wrestlers, professional athletes who were on the payroll of various princes, and the Japanese were very proud of them. Their champion, Koyanagi, was brought before the Commodore to be admired. Old Matt had to feel the bulging muscles, make suitable flattering remarks, and even punch the giant's paunch.

A ring was set up, and the Americans and their hosts retired to the porch of the treaty house to watch the wrestlers as they paired off for man-to-man combat. At first the two athletes circled each other, pawing the ground with their feet like bulls, looking for an opening. Then they crouched down, maneuvering carefully, and finally rushed at each other. The crash, as described in *Narrative*, "might have stunned an ox." Now they were locked in a straining hold, their faces turning red with the effort to throw one another. At last one would fall, with a heavy thud; the other would be declared the winner, and the loser would be helped from the ring. The day's festivities ended with a smart drill exhibition by the United States marines, after which the Japanese served a light meal of

A toast, one of many, is under way on the canopied deck of the Powhatan *during a banquet celebrating the success of negotiations. Perry's most elaborate social gesture of the expedition was said to be a noisy event "of very evident enjoyment on the part of the guests."*

fish, soup, and eggs—with, of course, the traditional sake.

Back on the ship, Williams wrote in his diary: "Indeed, there was a curious melange today here, a junction of east and west, railroads and telegraph, boxers and educated [athletes], epaulets and uniforms, shaven pates and night-gowns, soldiers with muskets and drilling in close array, soldiers with petticoats . . . all these things, and many other things, exhibiting the difference between our civilization and usages and those of this secluded, pagan people."

Not to be outdone as a host, Perry invited the Japanese commissioners to a party on the *Powhatan*. On the appointed day, March 27, they came aboard, as a flag bearing the shogun's crest and another bearing the coat of arms of Hayashi went up the halyards. Knowing that Japanese custom would not permit the commissioners to sit down with their countrymen of lower rank, the Commodore invited them into his cabin, while their aides, numbering about sixty, joined the lower-ranking American officers at tables set up beneath an awning on the quarter-deck. As the meal progressed and the wines flowed, Hayashi preserved his dignity, though he politely tasted every dish and sampled every wine. Matsusaki, on the other hand, proved to be the life of the party; he soon began to show the effects of all he had drunk, the *Narrative* notes, "and became very particularly happy."

Outside on the quarter-deck the scene was lively; the ship's band played throughout the banquet, toasts were exchanged, and even the heartiest eaters among the Americans were amazed at the amount of food their guests put away. After the meal, the tables were cleared and a group of sailors blacked their faces and put on a minstrel show that brought broad smiles even to Hayashi's sober face. As the Japanese were leaving, Matsusaki clasped the Commodore in a tipsy embrace (crushing Perry's new epaulets in the process) and repeated, in Japanese, "Japan and America, all the same heart." Lieutenant Preble, a witness to the scene, heard the Commodore say, "Oh, if he will only sign the Treaty he may kiss me."

Two days later the *Vandalia* and the *Southampton* returned with a favorable report on Shimoda, and on Friday, March 31, 1854, the Treaty of Kanagawa was formally signed. In addition to assuring safe refuge for Americans cast upon Japanese shores and opening the ports of Shimoda and Hakodate to trade, it provided for the appointment after eighteen months of an American consul, to reside permanently at Shimoda.

"Eureka! It is finished!" wrote Preble in triumph. "The great agony is over! . . . Even Old Bruin (i.e. the Commodore) would smile if he only knew how to smile." It had been done in less than a month, and whether or not he permitted himself a smile, Old Matt was a justly proud man.

In the preparation of their minstrel show, Perry's sailors exhibited considerable ingenuity, using homespun costumes and a U.S. flag for a backdrop. Here, a nine-man band, complete with guitars, banjo, tambourine, and a set of bones, bangs out a lively tune for the party aboard the Powhatan.

LIBRARY OF CONGRESS

After signing the treaty, Perry went to Shimoda, one of the two ports opened by the agreement. Above, an exercise of American troops is in progress on the grounds of a Shimoda temple.

6   THE OPEN DOOR

For Matthew Perry the Treaty of Kanagawa was a bittersweet triumph. The achievement, he knew, was great; yet no matter how successful, the Japan mission had been a long, arduous, and often frustrating campaign. Old Matt was practically sixty, and the strain of active duty was beginning to tell. Frequent attacks of rheumatism had left him weak and drawn. Above all, he was exhausted.

In December of 1853, four months after the end of the first voyage to Japan, Perry had asked to be relieved of his command as soon as possible. Lying in a sickbed in Macao, dictating to his son, the Commodore informed the Secretary of the Navy that his health was "greatly impaired," and that he desired to return home after an honorable treaty had been wrested from the Japanese. Then, duties fulfilled, he would sail for America—with the Secretary's permission. Near the end of his letter, Perry pointed

Hakodate was thrown into confusion by the Americans' arrival. In the sketch below, natives and sailors dash about in various directions. Perched on the roofs of all the houses, as fire precautions, are tubs of water and brooms.

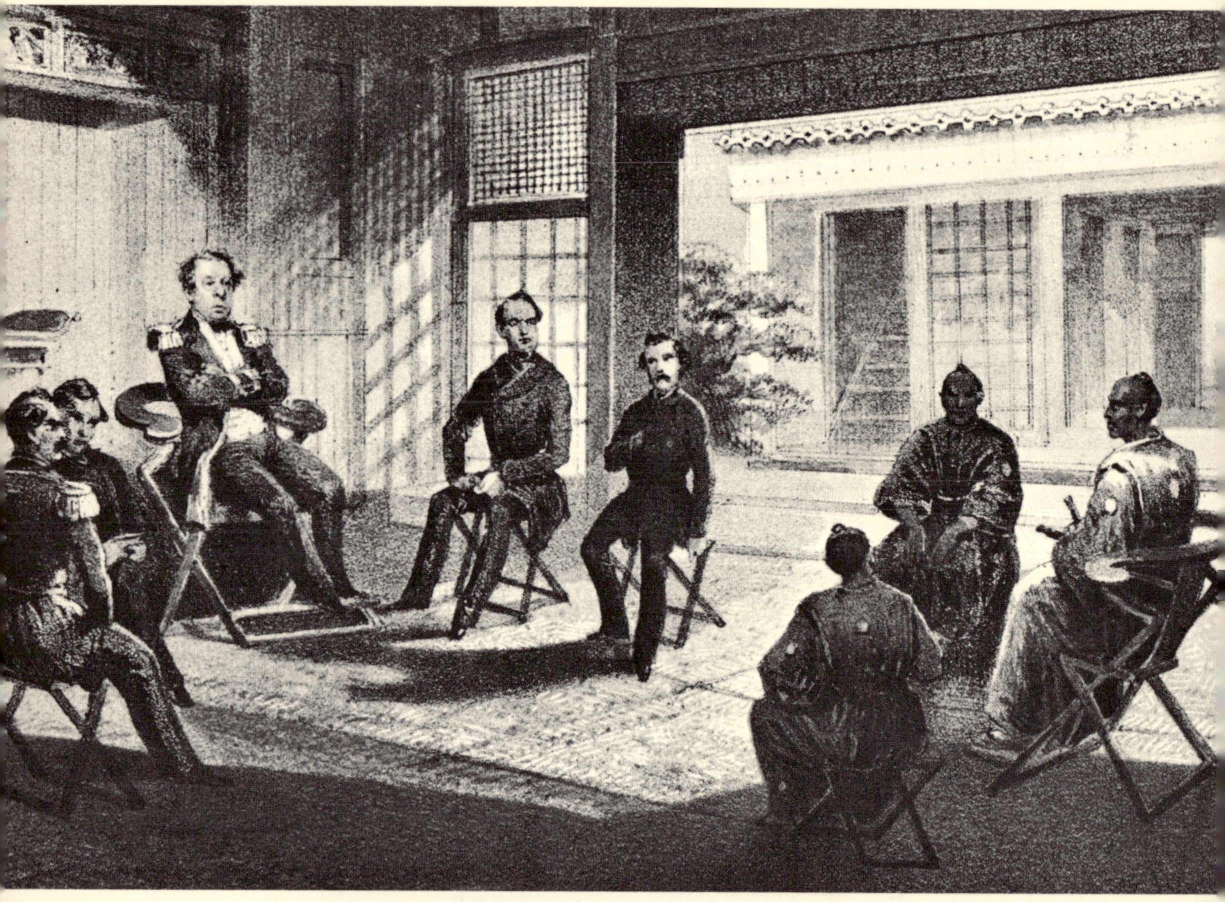

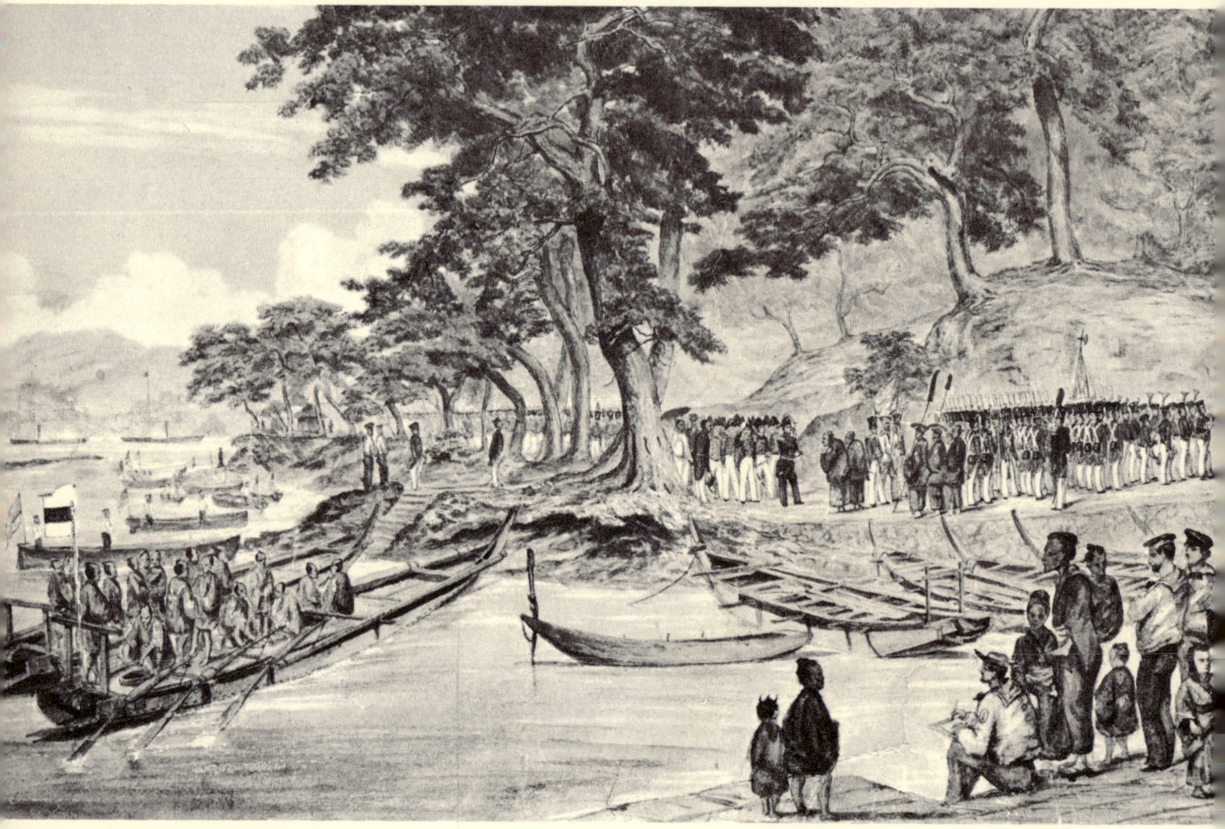

out that he had "seen more service than any other Captain in the Navy," and that in light of his record he might expect favorable treatment.

Now, on April 4, 1854—negotiations completed—the bands on the steamers were striking up "Old Folks at Home" and "Home Sweet Home," as the sloop *Saratoga* got under way for America. She carried copies of the treaty to be ratified by the Senate, and as she moved down Edo Bay, the crews of each remaining ship manned the rigging and raised three cheers. Aboard his flagship, the Commodore must have watched the scene grimly. A reply from the Navy Department had not arrived. Any disappointment he may have felt, however, was tempered by the prospects of what lay ahead. With a stern sense of duty, and not a little curiosity, he was prepared to inspect the two ports opened by the treaty.

To complete the inspection of Shimoda and Hakodate would take the squadron several months. From the beginning Perry and his officers were plagued by the cordial, yet stiff-willed resistance that had prevailed in nearly every encounter with the Japanese. The Americans were constantly shadowed by officials who took great

The Commodore is shown above conferring with Hakodate officials to set a boundary for American movement in the region. At left, Perry is seen landing at Shimoda to meet the imperial emissaries to whom the question of boundaries for both ports was referred.

125

The town and harbor of Hakodate and the rugged mountain country around it form a dramatic panorama as seen, at right, from the top of a nearby hill. There, a man looks out at Perry's squadron through a Japanese telescope —a bamboo tube fitted with lenses. The two women at the left were sketched by an American sailor at Shimoda.

pains to shield their people from the "barbarians."

Official word of the treaty had not even reached the remote provincial town of Hakodate, but the local government had heard rumors that the Americans were approaching. To forestall panic among the citizens, rules were issued to guide them in dealing with Perry's men. "All wine should be hidden," it was ordered, as well as any articles of value. The Americans were said "to like children very much . . . but if they should kidnap them it would be terrible. They notice women especially, so do not let them be seen while the ships are in port." Streets were to be barricaded and the fence along the beach made secure. Even the playing of musical instruments was forbidden.

The rumors and regulations threw the people into confusion. At first all the women were ordered out of town, but the roads became hopelessly clogged and the order had to be revoked. So many housewives rushed to stock up on rice that the price rose 13 per cent over night.

Although Perry was unaware of these local disturbances, he strongly protested against the practice of police surveillance that the Americans ran into at both ports. The treaty, he insisted, expressly permitted his men to walk about freely within a reasonable distance of the towns. Alternately bullying and flattering the officials, the Commodore gained concessions. He himself was taken on many sight-seeing excursions. Gifts, which the Commodore ultimately turned over to the Naval Museum and to the Smithsonian Institution, came in greater profusion than ever. On Perry's request, even a block of granite was furnished for the half-finished Washington Monument.

The fleet stopped at Shimoda twice, in mid-April and again in June. During the first visit, a sight-seeing party, which included Clerk Spalding of the *Mississippi*, was approached by a pair of richly dressed Japanese, each of whom wore the twin swords permitted only to those of high rank. One man stepped close to Spalding and pretended to admire his watch chain; then, furtively, he slipped a note inside the American's coat.

Spalding was able to make a quick translation of the Chinese inscription: "A secret communication, for the American men-of-war ships, to go up higher." The entire message revealed that the two Japanese were pro-Western scholars who wanted to accompany the fleet to America. After dark that night, they rowed out to the *Mississippi* in an open boat, cast it adrift, and clambered aboard.

All Perry's instincts told him to stow the two men below decks and keep their plan secret. But he knew that Japanese citizens were forbidden to leave the empire under penalty of death. If the Commodore expected the shogun to live up to the terms of the treaty, he could not very well take part in a plot to violate Japanese law. And possibly the two scholars had been sent to set just such a trap for

らうそく
世話いふ
さうり
ぬらり
文字
の桁
角文字と
あれほつるゝ
紀とろゝの

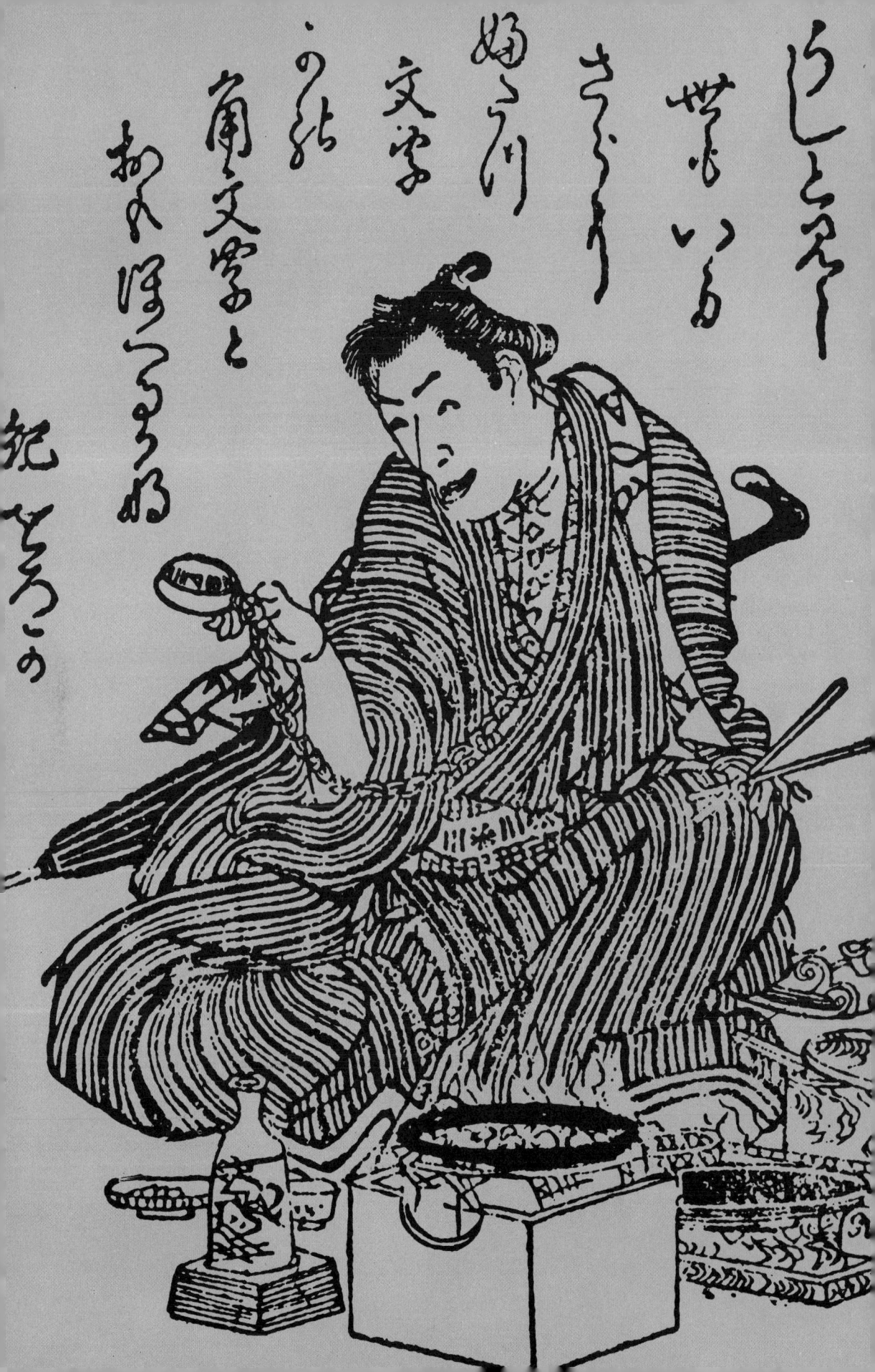

him. Reluctantly, Perry told them he could not do as they asked. He had them rowed ashore, where they were seen to disappear into the woods.

It had been no trap but a simple, if desperate, bid for freedom. A few days later other Americans on an outing ashore came upon the two unfortunate scholars, confined in a tiny cage. One of the captives found a piece of board and on it wrote a note in Chinese; then he handed it through the bars to his visitors. Translated, it read: "When a hero fails in his purpose, his acts are then regarded as those of a villain and a robber. In public we have been seized and pinioned and caged for many days ... Regarding the liberty of going through the sixty states [of Japan] as not enough for our desires, we wished to make the circuit of the five great continents ... Suddenly our plans are defeated, and we find ourselves in a half-sized house, where eating, resting, sitting and sleeping are difficult; how can we find our exit from this place? Weeping, we seem as fools; laughing, as rogues. Alas! for us; silent we can only be."

Perry attempted to intercede for the two prisoners. He was informed that the death penalty would not be invoked, and it was not; though regrettably one of the men died in prison. The other, placed under house arrest, lived until 1859, when he was beheaded for attempting to overthrow the shogun.

Aboard the *Mississippi*, Old Matt returned to Hong Kong in late July. Awaiting his arrival was a huge accumulation of mail, including the long-awaited instructions. The Navy Department, acceding to Perry's desires, had reviewed his request favorably. With the letter came warm congratulations from the Secretary of the

The poignant self-portrait at right, made in 1841—long before Perry's visit—shows a Japanese intellectual in manacles being told that he is to be executed for advocating Western ideas. Seventeen years after the Treaty of Kanagawa, the book illustration at left appeared; a young man openly enjoys novelties from the West—an umbrella, a pocket watch, and cooked beef.

FUJIMORI, *Kazan to Tamechika*

The two outstanding figures in America's early relations with Japan appear in these somber portraits. Above is a daguerreotype of Commodore Perry, taken in 1852. At right is a contemporary painting of Townsend Harris, America's resolute first consul to Japan.

Navy, who wrote, "You have won additional fame for yourself, [and] reflected new honor upon the very honorable service to which you belong. . . ."

Perry was free at last to return home, and when he set out on September 11 via commercial mail steamer, the officers and men of the *Mississippi* sent a message that must have warmed the old man's heart. "We shall never feel greater confidence, or stronger pride," it said, "than while under your command."

The Commodore arrived in the United States on January 12, 1855, two years and two months after he had steamed away for his rendezvous with destiny. Civic receptions were tendered in New York, in Boston, and in Newport, Rhode Island, his birthplace. In some quarters the gallant old sailor was compared with Columbus, da Gama, and Cook. When the *Mississippi* reached the Brooklyn Navy Yard in April, Perry went aboard to haul down his pennant, officially ending his mission to Japan.

American merchants heralded the the Treaty of Kanagawa as a master stroke of international diplomacy. It was, in the opinion of many men, a tremendous forward leap for United States trade relations in the Far East. Optimistic newspaper editors began publishing lists of goods desired by the people of Japan. On the surface it appeared as though the treaty had inaugurated a golden era for American business. By almost any gauge, how-

THE CITY COLLEGE, NEW YORK

Perry's return to the United States in 1855 is the theme of this sentimental picture of the passenger steamer Baltic, *in which he completed his voyage home. The print appeared in a portfolio illustrating the Japan expedition.*

ever, this feeling was premature and exaggerated.

The true success of Perry's expedition was more subtle and far-reaching. The Commodore set in motion forces that would define and advance the world position of the United States. Specifically, he forged a basis of naval and political strategy in Asia that has proved an invaluable legacy for American diplomats. As he saw it, the Open Door policy must guarantee the rights of Japan, or of any country to which it is applied, as well as the rights of Western nations.

The threat of imperialism in the Far East deeply concerned Perry. He was determined that the Open Door policy should not be limited to Japan but extended to most of the Pacific. Siam, Cambodia, Sumatra, Indochina, and parts of Borneo—each one of these places needed the "national friendship and protection" of the United States, Perry declared. He encouraged the Japanese to adopt methods of Western industrialization and technology, hoping they would free themselves of any real dependency on the West. Even before Old Matt departed for America, the Japanese were laying down plans for ocean-going ships.

In a very large sense the foundations of modern Japan were built by the combined efforts of Perry and pro-Western elements inside the empire. The Commodore's arrival had served to set free the boundless energies of the Japanese people. Mr. Dooley, a fictitious American newspaper character, later commented, "Whin we rapped on the dure, we didn't go in, they come out." Old Matt probably would have agreed.

The Commodore knew that only the first step had been taken in cementing Japanese-American relations. Valuable groundwork had been laid, but if it were to be permanent, the United States must pursue its opportunities. To this end Perry urged that Townsend Harris, formerly a New York merchant and shipowner, be appointed the first American consul at Shimoda.

Ironically, Harris' request to accompany the original expedition to Japan had been turned down. Undaunted, he applied for a diplomatic post in China; accepted, the fifty-year-old Harris distinguished himself as an astute, persevering envoy. On the basis of his record, he was appointed consul to Japan by President Franklin Pierce in 1855.

Harris took up his new duties in August of 1856, and there began one of the most remarkable diplomatic missions in American history. The American copies of the Treaty of Kanagawa specifically stated that a consul would be permitted to reside at Shimoda "provided that either of the two governments deem such an arrangement necessary"—but the Japanese made it obvious that Harris was unwelcome. Officials informed him that their version of the treaty said *both* governments had to agree upon the necessity, which in this case clearly did not exist. Moreover, a series of earthquakes and typhoons had struck the port since his arrival, and certain antiforeign elements regarded the disasters as divine disapproval of the Perry treaty.

The Japanese lied to Harris shamefully. They would not answer his letters. They ringed the consulate with armed guards. Worst of all, Harris was utterly neglected by his own government during the first stages of his mission. Fourteen months passed before he saw an American ship, and it was a full year and a half before he heard from the State Department.

Relying on his own resources—he had no squadron to help enforce his

COLLECTION OF TSUNEO TAMBA, YP-41

This Japanese painting shows Harris, wearing the diplomatic sash, accompanied by "American officials" in what is described as a conference room in Edo Palace. The meeting may have occurred after the signing of Harris' trade treaty, and the "officials" were probably Navy officers from an American ship in Edo Bay at the time.

Harris' consulate and home appear in his secretary's ink sketch below, behind what Harris called "the first Consular Flag ever seen in this Empire." These buildings are also partly visible in the 1860 engraving above, which shows the *Mississippi* anchored in Shimoda harbor.

demands—Harris gradually began to make headway. More than headway: on December 7, 1857, he was received by the shogun at Edo—not prostrating himself on the floor as the royal councilors did, not groveling as the Dutch had been forced to do for centuries, but standing erect and proudly making his speech of greeting. The Japanese, he wrote, were dumbfounded to see him "look the awful 'Tycoon' in the face, speak plainly to him, hear his reply—and all this without any trepidation, or any 'quivering of the muscles of the side.'"

Remaining at Edo, Harris virtually taught economics to the ministers of the shogun, helping them to set up a schedule of export and import duties; and with them he hammered out a mutually satisfactory trade treaty. On July 29, 1858, aboard the *Powhatan*, which had arrived in Edo Bay a month before, the treaty was formally signed.

For a comparable American diplomatic triumph one would have to go back to Benjamin Franklin in Paris on the eve of the Revolution. Like Franklin, Harris won the lasting esteem of his hosts; when he finally left Japan a prince of the empire said to him: ". . . I am sorry that there is nothing I can give you which is equal to the value of the help you have been to us. I wish I could give you Mt. Fuji, but I am sorry that it is impossible."

Harris' task had been complicated by unbelievable confusion at the highest level of Japan's government; bad enough at the time of Perry's second visit, the situation had grown steadily worse. The shogunate wore two faces. Toward foreigners it turned the face of friendship, for the most intelligent of the shoguns' advisers realized that the opening of the country could not be postponed. Pro-Western movements among the citizens were becoming infinitely more difficult to control. The advisers, trying to appease their most outspoken critics, had ordered a halt to the petty harassments that had made Harris' life at Shimoda so miserable.

The insecure shogunate felt obliged, however, to conceal this conciliatory attitude from its own people. Efforts were made to delude the people into thinking that the government was as opposed to admitting "barbarians" as it had ever been.

Caught in the web of his own deceptions, the shogun signed Harris' treaty without the approval of the emperor. It was a grave error; the insecure Tokugawa regime had demonstrated its inability to cope with the foreigners. Added impetus was given to a movement to restore the emperor to power. An opposition party, whose rallying cry was "Honor the Emperor and expel the barbarians," threatened to topple the shogunate and sweep the Westerners into the sea. Finally, in 1866, civil war broke out, and to aggravate the situation, the shogun died early in the fall of the same year.

His successor inherited a government stripped of power, an empty treasury, and the shattering effects of

In this Japanese painting, Emperor Meiji is being enthroned beneath an ornate canopy, his face hidden in accordance with ancient tradition. The date is October 12, 1868, a time of violent political change which had been brought about in part by the regime's inability to deal effectively with "barbarian" powers.

internal rebellion. After waiting a reasonable interval—some ten months—the new shogun resigned. Henceforth, it was ordered, Japan would be ruled only in the name of the emperor. To signal the change, Edo was given the new name of Tokyo, and there, following his ascension to power in 1868, Emperor Meiji was installed in the palace of the shogun.

Like much that had gone before it, the restoration of the emperor resulted from irrepressible forces within and without the empire. It had become obvious that the ancient dual form of government would no longer suffice in dealing with the formidable powers of the West. What had once functioned so well during the days of seclusion now was outmoded. The advocates of change believed that a strong, centralized government was necessary to place Japan on an equal footing in relations with the West. Were it not for Matthew Perry and Townsend Harris, however, the Meiji restoration might have been years longer in coming.

The Harris treaty had had immediate and serious ramifications for all of Japan; for much of America the results were almost as immediate, but of a far different nature. In 1860, while tensions were rising to a boiling point within the empire, a diplomatic mission was sent to the United States to exchange ratifications of Harris' treaty. It had been signed aboard the *Powhatan*, and it was deemed fitting that the *Powhatan* should carry the eighteen ambassadors and their fifty-three servants across the Pacific. Escorted by the Japanese ship *Kanrin Maru*, the steamer set out from Yokohama on February 13. In many respects she resembled a floating zoo more than a warship of the U. S. Navy. Crammed into her hold and overflowing onto the deck were fifty tons of luggage and gifts—including cattle, sheep, pigs, poultry, and representative Japanese art, in addition to the many personal effects of the ambassadors.

After a layover in Honolulu, where the Japanese saw their first billiard game and ate their first bananas, the *Powhatan* dropped anchor at San Francisco on March 29. The usual parades, banquets, and 17-gun salutes were impressive enough to the travelers, but apparently American social customs were most fascinating to them.

Perhaps the greatest novelty was an iced drink. Each Japanese seemed to have his own particular way of dealing with the problem of ice: some of the men actually swallowed it, others preferred to chew it, while still others deemed it best to spit it out. Dancing was also a curiosity to the members of the mission. One of them characterized the American custom as "hopping around the room together."

From San Francisco the *Powhatan* sailed to Panama, where a train was ready to carry the Japanese across the Isthmus. Finally, after transferring to another Navy ship, they arrived in

The Kanrin Maru, *one of Japan's first ocean-going ships, is pictured at right caught in a Pacific storm as it sails toward America on a mission to confirm Harris' treaty in 1860. Above, a box containing copies of the treaty is being paraded through New York in a wheel-borne pagoda. This screen is one part of a scroll painted by a member of the mission.*

Washington on May 14. Awaiting them was a stupendous celebration.

The roar of a 17-gun salute boomed across the water, a marine band "discoursed the most delightful melodies," and large American and Japanese flags were unfurled as the ambassadors' ship eased into its slip at the Washington Navy Yard. A milling, clamorous crowd of some 4,000 persons was on hand to greet the visitors; Congress was adjourned for the day, and most of the capital's high-ranking Army and Navy officers were present and so were scores of curious, gaping children.

Simultaneously, as the crowd was struggling for a glimpse of the visitors, several Japanese artists appeared on the deck to make sketches of the scene ashore. Franklin Buchanan, who had been fleet captain of Perry's expedition to Japan and who within two years was to become an admiral in the Confederate Navy, went aboard ship to give a welcoming address. Shortly afterward, an official photograph was taken, and then the entire assemblage embarked on a parade through the streets of Washington. Carried at the head of the procession was an elaborate red box, containing copies of Harris' treaty.

An estimated 20,000 people stood along the route; at times the jostling, pushing crowd broke through police lines and forced the parade to a halt. Despite the raucous reception, one newspaper correspondent considered the occasion "well-fitted to conciliate [the] regard and confidence of our illustrious visitors. . . ."

The Japanese were determined to get down to business quickly, and on

May 17, the ambassadors, accompanied by a color guard and a marine band, proceeded to the White House to present their credentials to the President. Accustomed to courtly ceremony, the Japanese must have been mortified by what they saw. High government officials were milling about, seeking decent vantage points—during the proceedings one senator and three ladies were seen to be standing on a single chair. Speeches were almost drowned out by the great noise. The affair dragged on for an hour and forty-five minutes before the stunned Japanese returned to their hotel.

Following a round of parties and receptions, the visitors were taken on a tour of the Capitol. "As we entered," one of the visitors recalled, a Congressman was "making a speech at the top of his voice. . . . There is no end to speakers . . . some speaking quietly, some wildly brandishing their arms. . . ."

Celebrations had also been organized in Baltimore, Philadelphia, and New York, and after departing from their Washington friends, one of the exhausted Japanese wrote in his diary: "We all wept. Seeing them also weeping, we realized they are a tender-

Foremost among the stern-faced figures in this photograph of the Japanese ambassadors and their hosts at the Washington Navy Yard are Shimmi Buzen-no-Kami, head of the mission, sitting third from right, and standing behind him, Franklin Buchanan, Perry's fleet captain.

hearted people." Even though the capital was girding itself for civil war, it had found time to honor and salute the representatives of Japan—the gesture was long remembered on the far side of the Pacific.

The seventy-one-man contingent arrived in New York on June 16, to be met by an even greater reception than that in Washington. At the Battery the Japanese received a thunderous salute, after which they joined an immense parade that took them to their hotel on Broadway. The high light of the visit came on June 25 with a grand ball that was characterized as "the finest public entertainment ever given in this country." It was reviewed with glowing accounts in the New York newspapers and indeed it should have been; preparations had been made for 10,000 dinner guests, and five bands were present for dancers. The musicians were instructed

President Buchanan received the ambassadors in the mobbed East Room of the White House. In this magazine illustration, his interpreter confers with him while the Japanese wait patiently to present the handsome treaty box. Three ladies have climbed on furniture, left, the better to see it all.

to play through the night if necessary. According to one account, 20,000 people managed to attend the grand festivities.

The Japanese were scheduled to depart for their homeland on June 30, but before doing so, Manjiro, who had come on the mission as a lesser envoy, journeyed to Fairhaven for a nostalgic reunion with the aging Captain Whitfield. The ambassadors did not have a chance to meet Commodore Perry. On March 4, 1858, four months before Townsend Harris succeeded in prying the door to Japan all the way open, Old Matt died. He had finally succumbed to the rheumatism contracted many years before as a young lieutenant with the Mediterranean squadron.

The Japanese, however, did call on the Commodore's widow. One of them, obviously moved by the event, wrote: "What a change in a few years! Today, six years after that great national crisis [Perry's second visit to Edo Bay], we are here in the midst of the friendly American nation, welcome guests in the home of the very Commodore Perry whose great fleet might have stirred our peaceful land into battle! The time has come when no nation may remain isolated and refuse to take part in the affairs of the rest of the world."

Commodore Perry's expedition had indeed insured that neither Japan— nor his own awakened country— would ever again close its doors to the rest of the world.

145

COLLECTION OF CARL H. BOEHRINGER

Japan had become so receptive to foreigners by 1879 that when ex-President Ulysses Grant visited Tokyo that year he was given the lavish entertainment shown here. Grant, wearing civilian clothes and a beard, and his wife, above, watch samurai demonstrate their skills.

AMERICAN HERITAGE PUBLISHING CO., INC.

PRESIDENT JAMES PARTON
EDITORIAL DIRECTOR JOSEPH J. THORNDIKE, JR.
EDITOR, BOOK DIVISION RICHARD M. KETCHUM
ART DIRECTOR IRWIN GLUSKER

AMERICAN HERITAGE JUNIOR LIBRARY

MANAGING EDITOR RUSSELL BOURNE
ART DIRECTOR EMMA LANDAU
ASSOCIATE EDITOR WADE GREENE
ASSISTANT EDITOR DENNIS A. DINAN
CHIEF PICTURE RESEARCHER JULIA POTTS GREHAN
PICTURE RESEARCHER MARY LEVERTY
COPY EDITOR PATRICIA C. FROME
EDITORIAL ASSISTANT MARY GLOYNE PAYNE
EDITORIAL ASSISTANT NANCY SIMON

ACKNOWLEDGMENTS

The Editors are deeply grateful to the owners and curators of several private and public collections in which Japanese and American art of importance to this book was found—particularly to Carl H. Boehringer, Executive Director, American Chamber of Commerce in Japan, Tokyo. Special thanks are also owed to members of the Perry family for their kind cooperation in locating pertinent materials: Mrs. Henry G. Bartol, Mrs. August Belmont, and the Reverend DeWolf Perry. Finally, the Editors wish to thank the following individuals and organizations for their assistance and for making available pictorial material in their collections:

Robert G. C. Fee, Newport News, Virginia
J. Welles Henderson, Philadelphia
The Mariners Museum—Agnes Brabrand
J. William Middendorf II, New York City
Arthur N. Miyazawa, Tokyo
New-York Historical Society—Arthur Breton
New York Public Library—Karl Kup, Curator of the Spencer Collection
Philadelphia Maritime Museum—John Jackson, Director
United States Naval Academy Museum—Captain Wade DeWeese, USN (Ret.), Director
Emily V. Warinner, Honolulu

The photograph on page 14 (top), from the Metropolitan Museum of Art, is the gift of I. N. Phelps Stokes, Edward S. Hawes, Alice Mary Hawes, and Marion Augusta Hawes, 1937.

FOR FURTHER READING

Barrows, Edward M. *The Great Commodore.* Bobbs-Merrill, 1935.

Cole, Allan B., editor. *With Perry in Japan: the Diary of Edward Yorke McCauley.* Princeton University Press, 1942.

Cross, Wilbur. *Naval Battles and Heroes.* American Heritage Junior Library, 1960.

Dulles, Foster R. *America in the Pacific.* Houghton Mifflin, 1938.

Graff, Henry F., editor. *Bluejackets with Perry in Japan.* New York Public Library, 1952.

Harris, Townsend. *The Complete Journal of Townsend Harris.* Charles E. Tuttle Co., 1959.

Ienaga, Saburo. *History of Japan.* Japan Travel Bureau, 1958.

Kaneko, Hisakazu. *Manjiro, The Man Who Discovered America.* Houghton Mifflin, 1956.

Sansom, George B. *The Western World and Japan.* Knopf, 1950.

Statler, Oliver. *The Black Ship Scroll.* Weathermark Editions, 1963.

Szczesniak, Boeslaw, editor. *The Opening of Japan; A Diary of Discovery in the Far East, 1853 1856.* University of Oklahoma Press, 1962.

Treat, Payson J. *Japan and the United States 1853–1921.* Houghton Mifflin, 1921.

Wallach, Sidney, editor. *Narrative of the Expedition of an American Squadron to the China Seas and Japan.* Coward-McCann, 1952.

Walworth, Arthur. *Black Ships Off Japan.* Knopf, 1946.

Warinner, Emily V. *Voyager to Destiny.* Bobbs-Merrill, 1956.

Index

Bold face indicates pages on which illustrations appear

A

Abe, Lord, 92, 99
Adams, Comdr. Henry A., 71, 73, 83, **95**, 106
Alleghany, 50
"American Anchorage," 83, 90, 92
Audubon, John James, 107, 115

B

Baltic, **132**
Bent, Lt. Silas, 50
Biddle, Com. James, 19–20, 47, 66
Bonin Islands, 60–61 (map), 64, 65

Brooklyn Navy Yard, **55**, 130
Buchanan, Capt. Franklin, 50, 54, 71, 73, 90, 140–141, **142–143**
Buchanan, Pres. James, **144–145**
Buzen-no-Kami, Ambassador Shimmi, **142–143**

C

California, 14, 36, 38
Canton, China, 17, 55
China, 7, 17, 18, 19, 46, 50, 53, 54, 81, 83, 86, 90, 106, 133
Chinnery, George, painting by, **17**

Christianity, 18–19, 24–27, 30, 32, 39, *see also* Missionaries
Clipper ships, 17, **17**
Colt, Samuel, 54, 107
Columbus, 20, **21,** 47
Contee, Lt., 69, 70
Cooper, Capt. Mercator, 19, 47
Council of Elders, 30

D

Daimyos, 30, 40, 43
Deshima, Japan, 30, 32, 33, **36–37, 38, 40–41**
Dutch, the, 30, 33, **38, 40–41,** 53, 100, 113, 137
 Opperhoofd, 33, 65

E

Edo (Tokyo), Japan, 19, 30, 33, **33,** 66, 72, 73, 87, 113, 115, 137, 139
Edo Bay, 19, **21, 22, 74–75,** 81, **82,** 83, 90, 125, 137
Emperor, Japanese, 27, 30, 92, 137, 139, *see also* Mikado
England, *See* Great Britain
Everett, Alexander, 19

F

Fillmore, Pres. Millard, **15,** 54, 58
 Letter to Emperor of Japan, **68,** 69–70, 72, 73–74, 80, 81, 90, 100, 106
France, 46, 86
Franklin, 36

G

Gadsden, James, 14
Glynn, Comdr. James, 20, 47, 50
Grace, 19
Grant, Pres. Ulysses S., **146–147**

Great Britain, 7, 14, 33–34, 43, 46, 53

H

Hakodate, Japan, 115, 118, **122–123, 124–125,** 125, 126, **127**
Harris, Townsend, **131,** 133, **135, 136,** 137, 139, 141, 145
Hawaiian Islands, 16, 18, 34, 36, 38, 139
Hayashi, 97, 99, 100, 102, 106, **109,** 113, 115, 118
Healy, G. P. A., painting by, **15**
Heine, Wilhelm, 89
 paintings by, **front endsheet, 58–59, 80**
Hideyoshi, 27, 30
Hokkaido, Japan, 115
Hong Kong, China, 17, **17,** 54, 86, 129
Honshu, Japan, 115

I

Ido, "Prince of Iwami," 80, 81
Ido, "Prince of Tsus-shima," 98
Isawa, "Prince of Mema-saki," 98

J

Jackson, Pres. Andrew, 19
Japan, 60–61(map)
 Government, 27, 30, 32, 33, 40, 43, 46, 47, 92, 93, 118, 137, 139
 Trade, 24, 30, 32, 33, **36–37, 38,** 100, 102, 106, 118, 132, 137
Jefferson, Pres. Thomas, 14, 34
John Howland, 34, 36, **43,** 53

K

Kagoshima, Japan, 24
Kanagawa, Japan, **84–85, 86,** 87, **87, 88,** 90, 92, 97, 113, 115

151

Kanrin Maru, 139, **141**
King, Charles W., 19, 46
Komei, Emperor, **13**
Kyoto, Japan, 27, 30

L

Lady Washington, 19
Lewis, John, 50
   sketch by, **86**
Lewis, Lawrence, 50
Lexington, 86, 87
Loochoo Islands, *See* Ryukyu Islands

M

Macao, China, 55, 86, 122
Macedonian, 50, 87
Manhattan, 19, 20, 47
"Manifest Destiny," 14, 16, *see also* California, Hawaiian Islands
Manjiro, 34, 36, 38–40, 47, 53, 145
Marines, U. S., 11, 62, 63, 70, 76, **77**, 80, 89, **92**, **98–99**, **101**, 109, 116
Matsusaki, 98, 118
McCauley, Edward Yorke, sketches by, **72–73**, **82**, **114**
McLane, R. M., 86–87
Meiji, Emperor, **138**, 139
Meiji restoration, 137–139
Mexican War, 14, 39, 49, 50, 51, 100
Mikado, 27, **32**, 54, *see also* Emperor
Missionaries, 18, **18**, 24–27, **24–25**, **27–28**, 30, 55
   Franciscans, 30
   Jesuits, 24–25, 30
Mississippi, 7, 11, **48**, 49, 50, **51**, 54, **56–57**, 58, 65, 66, 73, 75, 87, 127, 129, 130, **136**
Morrison, 19, 46, 55
Mt. Fuji, **22**, 66, 137
Mung, John, *See* Manjiro

N

Nagasaki, Japan, 7, 24, **24–25**, **28–29**, 30, 33, **37**, 39, 43, 65, 70, 72, 73, 81, 100, 106, 113
Naha, Okinawa, 58, 59, **58–59**, 62, 63, 64, 65
Naval Academy (Annapolis), 49, 50
Navy, U. S., 11, 12, 17, 20, 49, 50, 54, 69, 72, 125, 129–130, 139
"No Second Thought" order, 46

O

Okinawa, 39, 58–65
Open Door policy, 132
Opium War, 46

P

Peale, Rembrandt, painting by, **53**
Perry, Com. Matthew Calbraith, **cover, title page**, **9**, **13**, **48**, **52**, **58**, **70**, **77**, **93**, **94**, **101**, **124**, **130**
   Early career,
      Brooklyn Navy Yard, 55
      Mexican War, 14, 49, 50, 51
      Naval Academy, 49
   Expedition to the Orient, 60–61 (map)
      Preparation, 50, 53, 54
      Departure, 49, 54
      China, 54–55, 58, 83, 86, 87, 122, 129
      Japan, 1853, 11, 12, 67–83
      Japan, 1854, 89–118, 127, 129
      Ryukyu Islands, 58–65, 83
      Return to U.S., 130
      Results of expedition, 131–133, 139, 145
   Character, 53, 76, 82, 100, 131
   Death, 145
   Health, 122
   Reputation, 49, 50, 55, 107
Perry, Oliver Hazard (brother), 53, **53**
Perry, Oliver Hazard (son), 53, 55, **95**, 122
Pierce, Pres. Franklin, 133

Plymouth, 11, 50, 54, 58, 65, 66
Portman, H. A. L., 69, **95**, 97
Powhatan, **87**, 99, **117**, 118, **119**, 137, 139
Preble, 20, 47, 50
Preble, Lt. George, 115, 118
Princeton, 50, 54

R

Roberts, Capt. Edmund, 19
Russia, 7, 43, 86
Ryukyu (Loochoo) Islands, 39, 58–65, 60–61 (map), 81, 83, 87

S

Saberosuke, Nagashima, 69, 70, 72, 75, 80, 81, 90
Samurai, 30, **35**, 40, 43, **146–147**
San Francisco, California, **12–13**, 38, 139
Sarah Boyd, 38
Saratoga, 11, 50, 54, 58, 65, 66, 87, 125
Sealing grounds, **16**, 17
Seward, Sen. William H., 19
Shanghai, China, 17, 55, 58, 86
Shimoda, Japan, 115, 118, **120–121**, **124–125**, 125, 127, 133, **136**, 137
Shoguns, 27, 30, **31**, 32, 33, 40, 43, 46, 47, 65, 72, 90, 92, 93, 115, 118, 127, 129, 137, 139, *see also* Tokugawas
Singapore, China, 65
Southampton, 50, 87, 115, 118
Spalding, Clerk J. W., 127
Sproston, John Glendy, sketches by, **101, 102**
Supply, 50, 54, 58, 65, 87
Susquehanna, 11, 12, 20, 50, 54, 55, 58, 62, 64, 65, 66, 69, 70, **71**, 75, 83, 87, 90, 113

T

Taylor, Pres. Zachary, 39

Toda, "Prince of Idzu," 80, 81
Tokugawa, Shogun Ieyasu, 30
Tokugawas, 30, 40, 43, 93, 97, 137
Tokyo, Japan, *see* Edo, Japan
Treaty of Kanagawa, 118, 122, 126, 130, 133

U

Udono, 98
Uraga, Japan, 66, **66–67**, 69, **69**, 70, 71, 72, 74, 81, 83, 98

V

Vandalia, 50, 87, 89, 115, 118
Vermont, 50
Vincennes, 20, **21**, 47

W

Washington, D. C. 140–142
Washington Monument, 127
Washington Navy Yard, 140, **142–143**
Webster, Daniel, **14**, 18, 54
Westward expansion (U.S.), 14, 16, *see also* California, Hawaiian Islands
Whalers, 16, 17, 53
Whitfield, Capt. William H., 34, 36, 145
Williams, Samuel Wells, 55, 58, 63, 69, 74, 77, 81, 83, **95,** 97, 98, 107, 113, 118
Wrestlers, sumo, **112, 114,** 116

X

Xavier, Francis, 24, **26**

Y

Yezaimon, Kayama, 71, 72, 73, 74, 75, 80, 81, 90, 97
Yokohama, Japan, 139

153

二月十日
武州横濱
人接應之圖

先時之圖一笠及版權所有者編
輯兼發行者大日本東京市本
所區相生町五丁目廿一番地
秋山亦太郎